The Basics of Turning Spirals

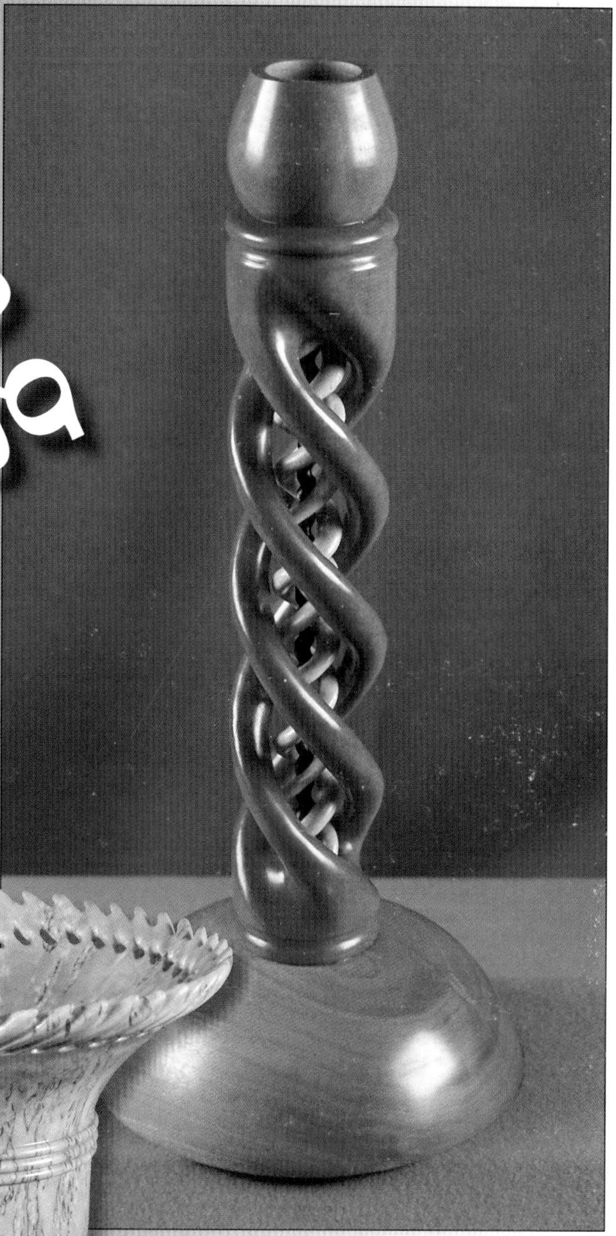

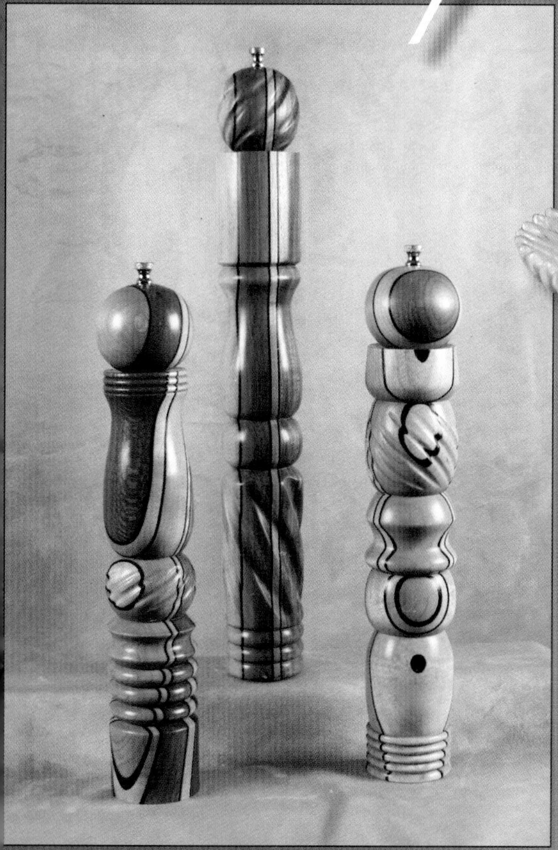

Bill Bowers

Schiffer® Publishing Ltd
4880 Lower Valley Road, Atglen, PA 19310 USA

Dedication

To Susan
For her patience in tolerating
my many idiosyncrasies for 36 years

and

To Meggie
Whose presence, paws on the keyboard or head on my
hand while I typed and edited pictures or manuscript
made the task most challenging and memorable

CONTENTS

Other Schiffer Books on Related Subjects:

Segmented Wood Turning, William Smith, $14.95
Turning Threaded Boxes, John Swanson, $14.95
Basic Bowl Turning, $12.95
Turning Ornaments & Eggs, Dick Sing, $14.95
Pens from the Wood Lathe, Dick Sing, $14.95
A Turner's Guide to Veneer Inlays, Ron Hampton, $14.95

Library of Congress Control Number: 2006929460

Designed by Mark David Bowyer
Type set in Aldine721 BT / Korinna BT

ISBN: 0-7643-2592-2
Printed in China

Published by Schiffer Publishing Ltd.
4880 Lower Valley Road
Atglen, PA 19310
Phone: (610) 593-1777; Fax: (610) 593-2002
E-mail: Info@schifferbooks.com

For the largest selection of fine reference books on this and related subjects, please visit our web site at **www.schifferbooks.com**
We are always looking for people to write books on new and related subjects. If you have an idea for a book please contact us at the above address.

This book may be purchased from the publisher.
Include $3.95 for shipping.
Please try your bookstore first.
You may write for a free catalog.

In Europe, Schiffer books are distributed by
Bushwood Books
6 Marksbury Ave.
Kew Gardens
Surrey TW9 4JF England
Phone: 44 (0) 20 8392-8585; Fax: 44 (0) 20 8392-9876
E-mail: info@bushwoodbooks.co.uk
Website: www.bushwoodbooks.co.uk

PROEM

When approached by a publisher about writing a book on turning I was somewhat surprised but highly complimented and most pleased. The impetus and inspiration for the book came from several articles on spiral turning published in Woodturning Design magazine over the past few years. If you please, indulge me the brief interlude as to how I became a turner, writer, and photographer—there may be some doubts concerning the later.

Reared in Pennsylvania, I was always intrigued by wood working but had no formal training other than watching my father work with hand tools when I was a very small child. Most of my joinery pieces were constructed in a haphazard fashion and would have aptly qualified as neanic.

As a teenager I attended the University of Pittsburgh obtaining degrees in mathematics, chemistry and produced a 120 page thesis in fine arts—questionable proof of artistic prowess. After the Pittsburgh stint I studied medicine in Philadelphia and returned to my hometown, Johnstown, Pennsylvania, to begin a medical residency. Not too far into the program I was drafted and sent to Fort Richardson, Alaska where I fought the Viet Nam War. It wasn't so bad as no gun fire or tropical climes bothered me for the three years. In my spare time I frequented the base's woodshop where my endeavors became the major entertainment for NCOs on evening duty. I constructed a kitchen table which had 4 completely differently turned walnut legs and enough beefiness to hold a car. The table still stands in my daughter's kitchen and has become quite a conversation piece—good or bad?

After Fort Richardson I returned to Pittsburgh where I completed my residency in internal medicine followed by a fellowship in gastroenterology. My family, wife Susan and daughter Suzanne moved with me back to Anchorage, Alaska, where I practiced gastroenterology for some 25 years. During that time, besides writing medical articles, editing a medical journal and photographing most of Alaska south of the Brooks range, I bought a Sears lathe and diligently turned all sorts of awfully made wood projects in my garage—most of which were used for firewood—and inspired my wife to become an expert wood critic able to spot "seconds" at a distance of 50 paces.

When Susan's mother came to live with us (fortunately she was not a wood critic) we needed a bigger house and of course I got to build a real shop, buy more tools and bigger and better lathes. The Powermatic 91 was my next lathe but shortly after purchasing it I bent the shaft. My good friend Arnie, a retired industrial arts teacher who could fix anything, was summoned to repair the mishap. Standing off to one side he queried me as to how I bent the 18 inch long, 1-1/2 inch diameter shaft and burned out the bearings which were adequately made for most trucks. I explained how I was turning a 70 pound stock of wet beech when the catastrophe ensued. Arnie asked me to take the same stance with my gouge. Appalled, he immediately stepped back and exclaimed, "You never took woodshop, did you?" My answer was a resounding "No." I had been scraping everything for 3 to 4 years and sanding it smooth or so it seemed.

Arnie recommended classes at Provo, Utah—Craft Supply USA—where I took my first with Ray Key. It was amazing how easy turning became when approached correctly. Later on I studied with Richard Raffan, Rude Olsonik, Allan and Stuart Batty, Mike Mahoney, Hans Weissflog, Stuart Mortimer (the true master of spiral turning), and a host of others. In fact, whenever our local wood turning club, of which I became the Grand Hegemon, sponsored symposiums and classes, I was allowed to be chief helper.

In 2000 I took an early retirement from the busy, stressful life of gastroenterology to become a full-time wood turner happily working as long as 12 hours a day, 7 days a week in my shop on the Oneway lathes I had acquired. With that much practice time I was determined to become proficient.

My interests include all forms of turning but especially one-of-a-kind artistic pieces. I like to go where no turner has gone before—some turners feel I should stay there—but it is sometimes difficult as new ideas are few and far between. In fact not much new has been tried since Jacob and Charles Holtzapffel's original works.

Subtle forms, curves, and shapes of nature are my inspirations and I like producing pieces people can't resist touching or picking up. After all, the results of turning are truly tactile expressions.

To those many instructors I've had in the past I say thank you for your patience. To those who feel I've copied their ideas or work I apologize. Picasso once said great students imitate their masters, the gifted ones copy them.

And with that brief introductory discourse we start the incunabula of spiral turnings by Bill Bowers.

CHAPTER 1

THE BASICS

The term "spiral turning" is actually a misnomer, as a paucity of turning is involved. Most of the work is accomplished using rasps, files, microplanes, planes and a host of various power tools while the lathe is turned off. It is a very old technique utilized in production of treasured antiques found more often across the pond then here in the states. At first, instructions may seem like the pseudo-aphorism of three blind men describing an elephant, but further observation as well as contemplation reveals an easily understood explanation. The process is simple enough to allow individuals completing Turning 101 classes to comprehend and accomplish the task.

As with any wood working skill safety first must be considered. Some sort of face and eye protection (helmet with face shield) must be utilized. No loose fitting clothes, jewelry, watches, or long hair should be worn. All these could lead to a catastrophe if caught in the lathe or chuck.

Some sort of dust collection should be utilized, be it a cyclone, bagged impeller system, or a micropore filter system. Ear protection is necessary when power tools or noisy filtering systems are operating.

The turning portions of the production require razor-sharp tools and a proficiency at keeping them in that state. A good reliable lathe at the proper height (spindle at elbow level) as well as comfortable supportive shoes to combat fatigue is necessary. Remember alcohol, sedative drugs, and power tools don't mix either.

Adequate lighting to observe subtleties of the work piece creates a better finished product. Proper abrasives and stable finishes are required. Selections of adequate timbers permit one to construct beautiful as well as stable spiral turned objects.

So what tools are needed besides the standard turning tools? Several round microplanes—large, medium, and small (yellow handle right to left)—obtainable from various wood craft or hardware stores; round rasps—1/16 inch, 1/8 inch, and 3/16 inches (red handle left to right); Stanley 92 shoulder plane (far right), Lie Nielson bronze 1/2 inch shoulder plane (far left) or a small hobby plane.

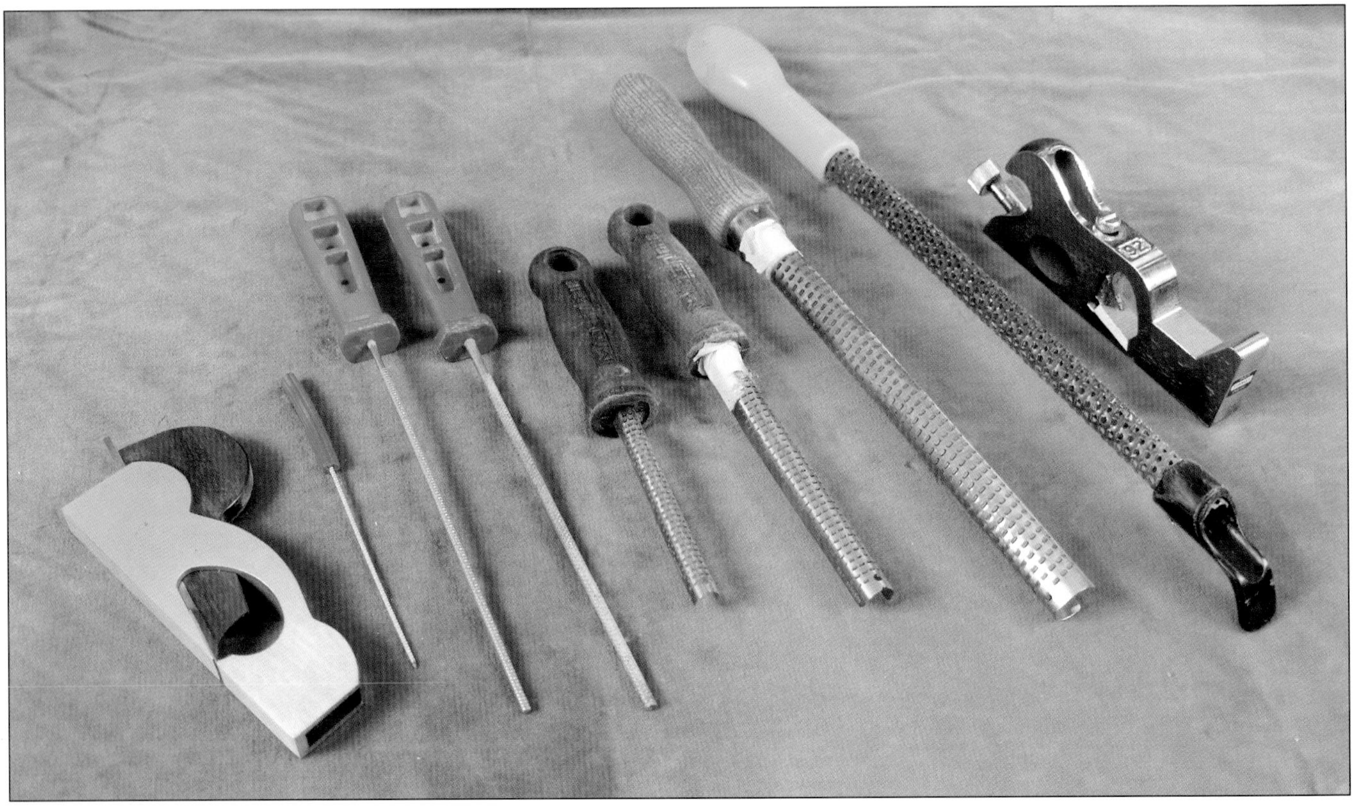

A variety of round files 1/8 inch to 1/2 inch, from coarse to fine are needed; and finally, variously sized long drill bits, 3/16 inches to 1 inch are required. Flexible abrasives (Vitex tearable sheets or Klingspor tearable yellow rolls) that can be rolled into ropes and home made sanding sticks that look like the slats out of old-fashioned blinds are needed as well. With these basic tools we are ready to start spiral turning.

Selecting the proper timber is necessary for the novice spiral turner. One should use a softer domestic wood such as pine, birch, maple or cherry without knots or other defects. Lighter pigmented wood allows drawn colored guide lines to be more discernable. Any size blank could be utilized, but try a 12-inch long 2 by 2-inch stock between centers turned to a cylinder. This should yield a cylinder about 1-3/4 inches in diameter 11-3/4 inches long after the ends are squared. I like to turn a dowel or spigot (3/4 inches in diameter) at either end about 1/2-inch long to be used to glue into a base and top later on. If a candlestick for tapers is being constructed one may wish to alter the length, fashioning the taper's candle cup.

At the ends of the cylinder turn a bead and cove with the bottom (headstock end) slightly broader than the top (tailstock end). This gives a better proportional appearance if the bottom bead and cove are 3/8 inches wide and the top is 1/4 inch wide. The turned spiral should fade into the top and bottom coves presenting a pleasant transition.

Using a lathe that has an indexing system is most helpful but home-made indexing systems may be easily constructed. If neither are available start lines may be determined by dividing pi (3.14159) times diameter (1.75 inches) by 2 for a single twist, 4 for a double, 6 for a triple, or 8 for a quadruple, etc. to find the circumferential distances. The start lines are always double the number of spirals. If you don't wish to do the calculations dividers can be randomly utilized to obtain approximate distances on the circumference for the start lines.

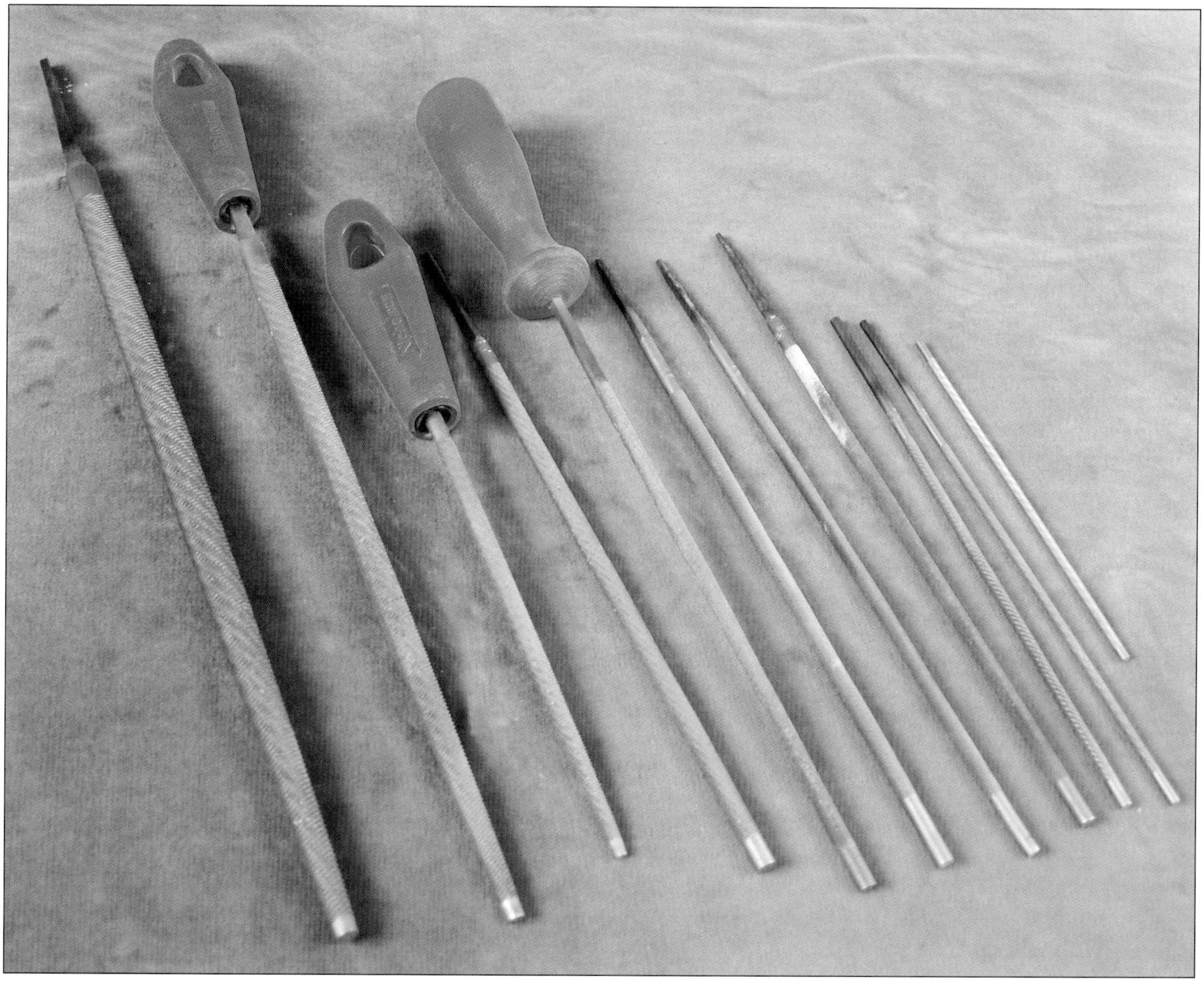

Double Barley Twists

An easy, pleasing spiral to begin with is the double barley twist—named after an English twisted candy cane. After the cylinder is turned, beads and coves turned at the ends, turn off or unplug the lathe.

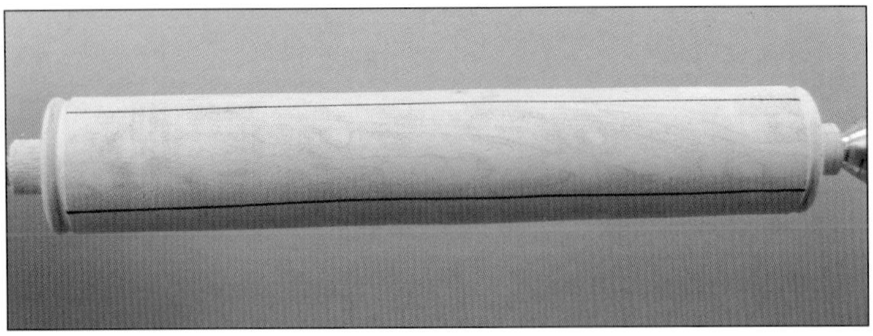

Mark four longitudinal (horizontal) lines on the turned cylinder from cove to cove using the lathe's indexing system. On a 48 point index the start lines would be at 12, 24, 36, and 48. If you start at 1 then the lay-out would be 1, 13, 25, and 37 on the index for four equidistant lines. Using the tool rest as a straight edge at dead center height draw the 4 start lines. [Please note that lines are drawn with a Sharpie marking pen for illustrative and photographic purposes only. In reality the standard Sharpie markers will bleed deeply into the wood presenting problems sanding out the dye on projects.]

The spiral's degree of slope steepness, grade, or pitch is considered next. The pitch usually looks best if it is twice the diameter of the piece, but oft times steeper or less steep inclines may be utilized for artistic effects. Also it is pleasing to the eye if the spirals make at least 2 complete revolutions. There are exceptions to the rule, however, when poetic license is issued.

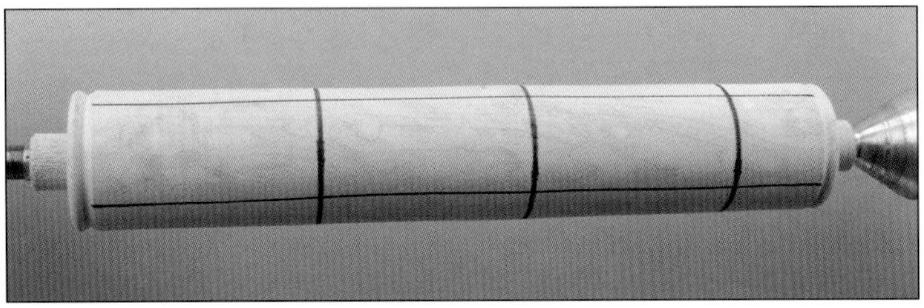

Draw a circumferential line 3 inches from the broad cove (left side of the cylinder). Draw a second pitch line 3 inches to the right of the first and a third 3 inches to the right of the second line as well. There are now 3 pitch lines in dark green.

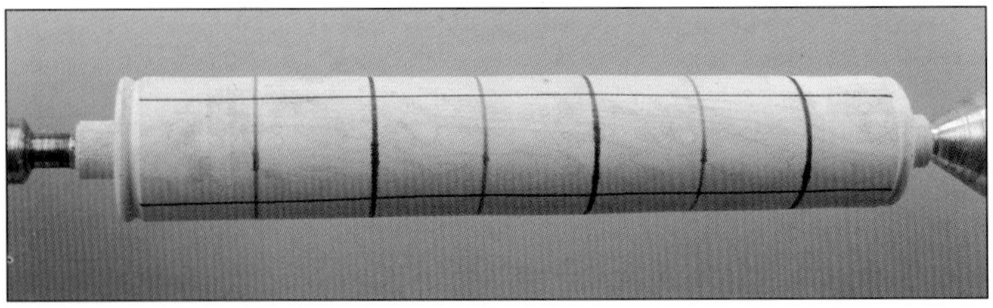

Divide each partition in half (six 1[illegible] inch segments) noted in light green and dark green.

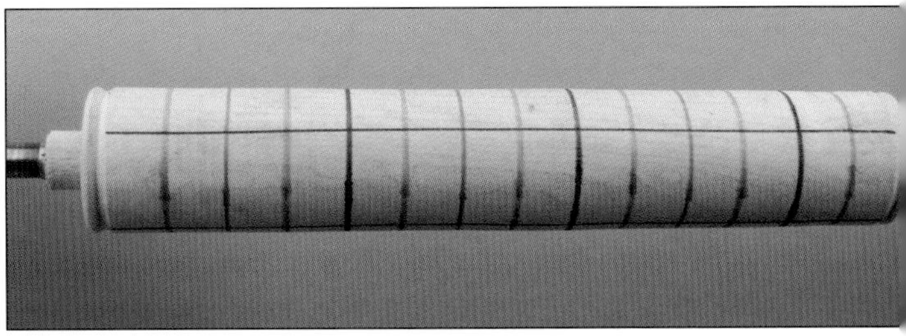

Divide each of those in half (fourteen 3/4 inch segments).

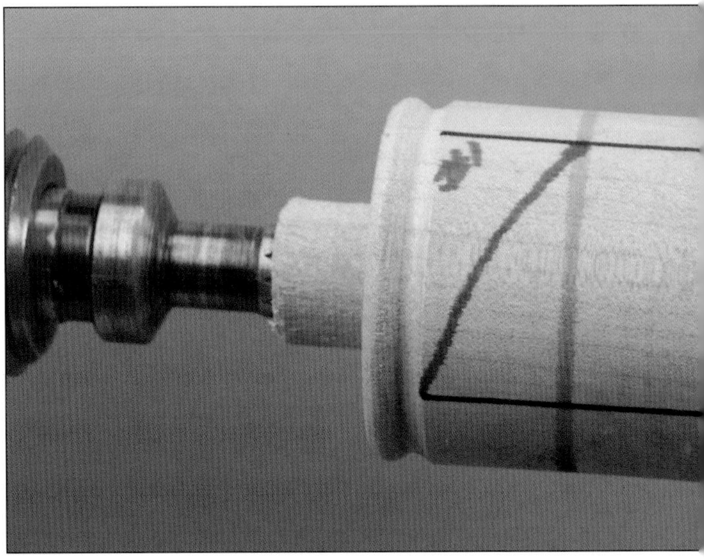

Mark #1 in any rectangle at the headstock, rotate the cylinder skipping a rectangle and mark #2. The designated rectangles are the starting points for a left-handed double barley twist. Had you wished to make a right-handed twist you would have started at the right-hand side or tailstock end. With a colored marker (preferably a colored pencil or other marker that won't bleed into the stock—I like to use gel pens) draw a diagonal baby blue line in rectangle #1 from the lower left hand corner to the upper right hand corner.

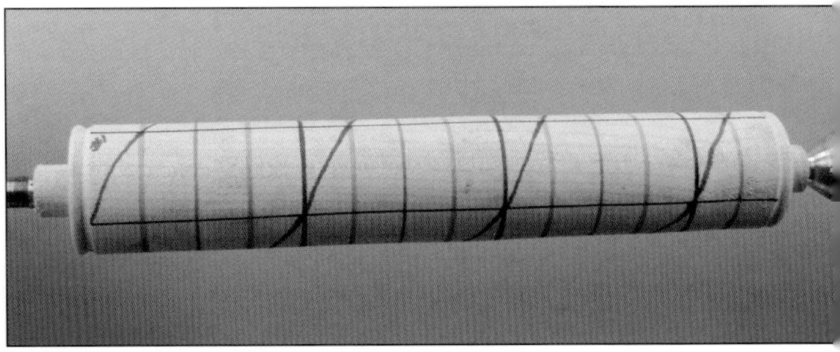

Continue the diagonal line into the next rectangle and all the way serially to the tailstock end.

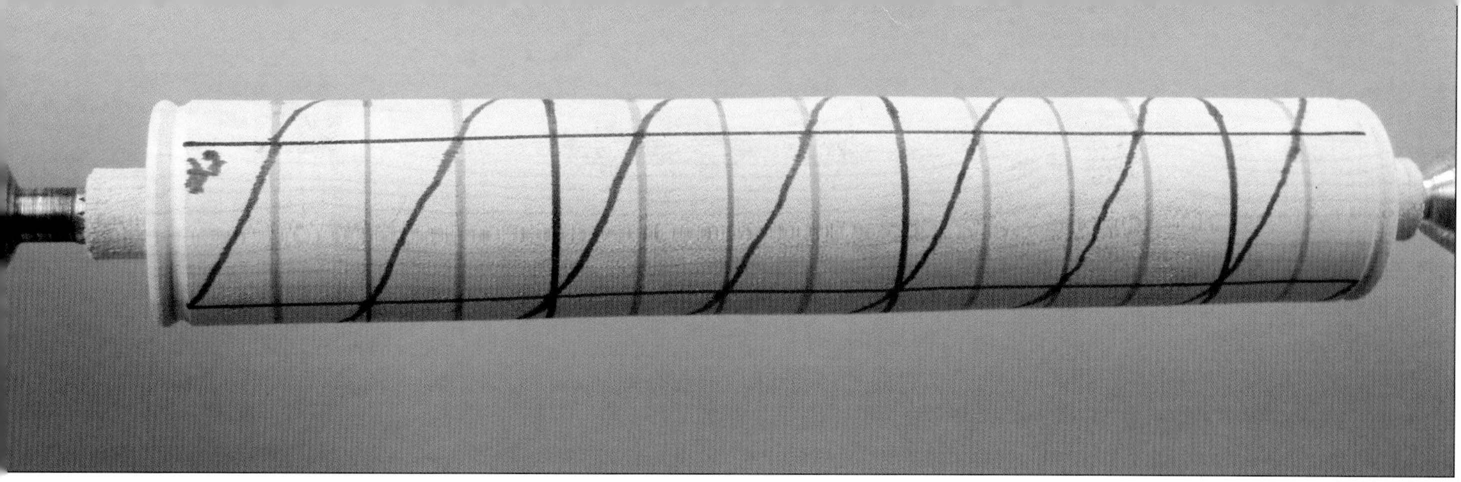

Do the same for rectangle #2 with the same baby blue gel pen.

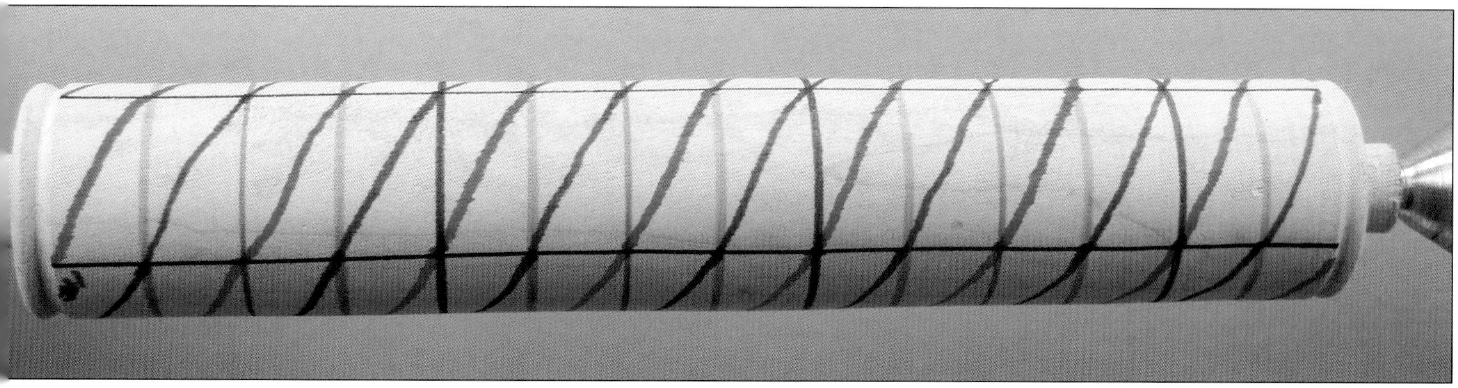

Next draw a diagonal line in the rectangle between #1 and #2 with a different colored marker (fluorescent pink) all the way around to the tailstock. Do the same for the rectangle between #2 and #1 with the same marker. The baby blue lines are the bines or top surface of the twists and the fluorescent pink lines are the cut lines or cove bottoms between the twists.

To form the coves, a kerf cut with an end grain cross cut or dovetail saw helps guide the microplane. (Some turners use a hand gouge but I find the microplane is easier to control.) If you place some duct tape 1/4 inch above the saw's teeth it will act as a good depth gauge in cutting. Cut from bottom (headstock) op (tail-stock) along the two fluorescent pink cut lines making a 1/4 inch deep kerf as the cylinder is hand-rotated.

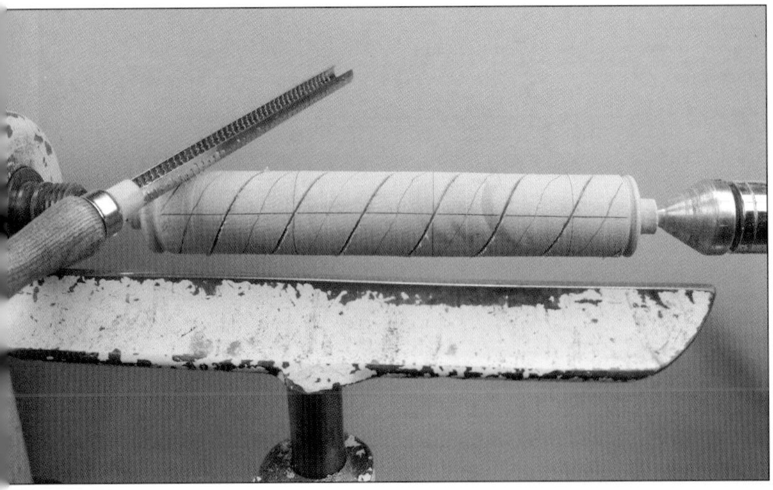

Use the large round microplane to rasp out the coves between the bine lines, taking care to be equidistant between bines. (Whenever the microplane fills with shavings lightly tap the end on the lathe bed while holding the microplane perpendicularly.)

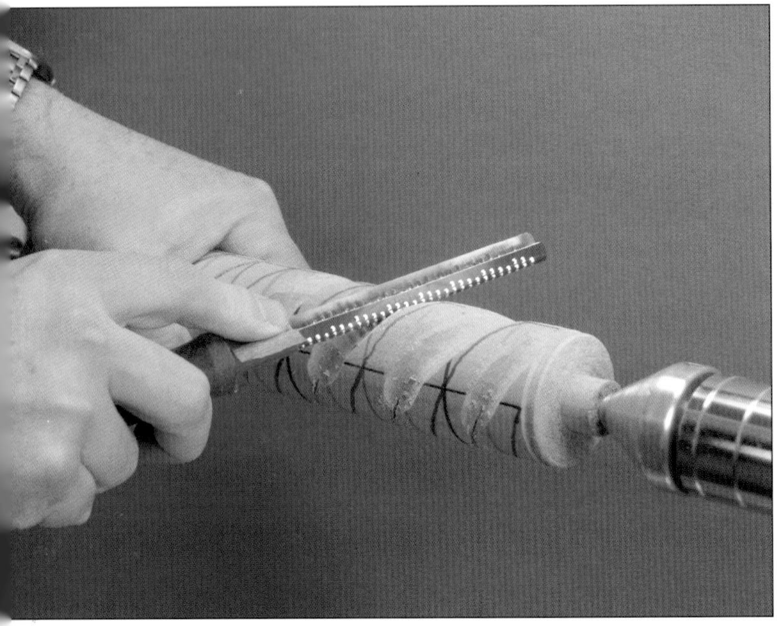

I usually lock the spindle and cut each parallel cove successively. I then unlock and rotate the cylinder slightly to another locked position so that smooth continuous parallel coves and bines can be fashioned. Don't try to remove all the waste material at once but carefully remove small amounts as you rotate and lock the spindle. If you are using exotics instead of soft woods the round microplane will dull quickly and will need to be replaced with a new one. It is also a good idea to wrap the proximal end of the microplane with tape to prevent cutting your index finger. Green self-sticking gauze is also good to wrap the thumb, index, middle and ring fingers (on both hands) when rasping or sanding.

After several trips around the coves with the round microplane and smooth coves are fashioned it is time to round over the bines. I use a small hobby plane or shoulder plane. One must remember to plane so as to give maximum support of wood fibers otherwise tear-out will occur.

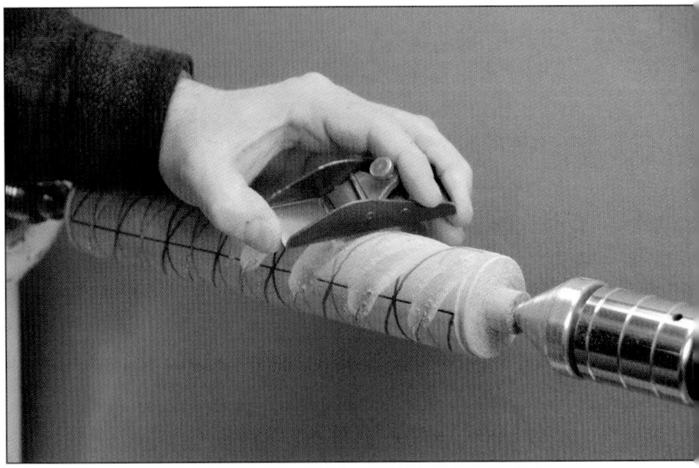

Remember plane on the left side of a left-handed twist bine from right to left toward yourself.

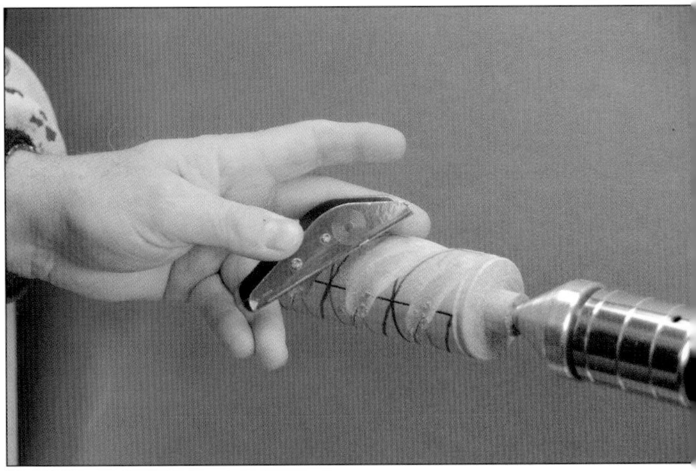

On the right side of a left-handed twist bine plane from left to right away from yourself.

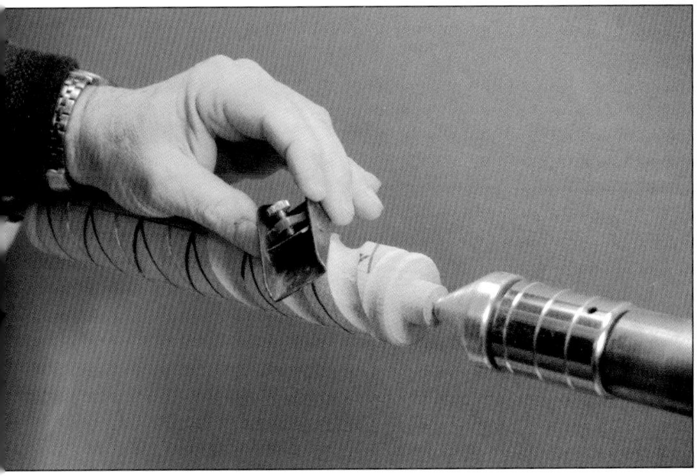

For a right-handed twist, plane on the left side of the bine right to left away from yourself.

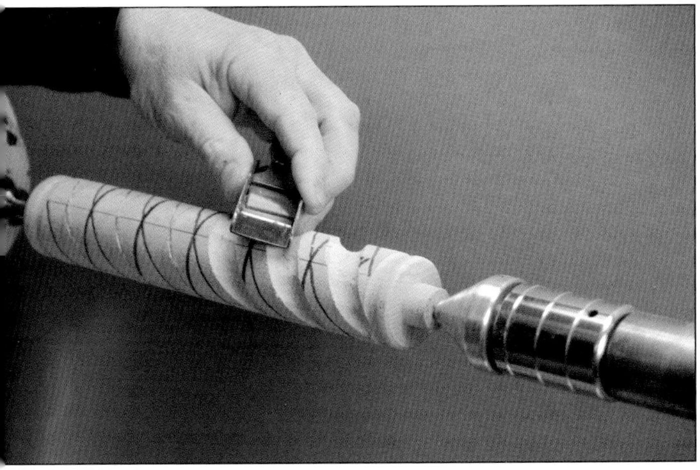

On the right side of the bine, plane left to right towards yourself.

After the bines are rounded over, a medium microplane can be used to deepen the cove, but be careful not to make linear gouges or marks. Various files from coarse to fine can be used to smooth out the coves and bines.

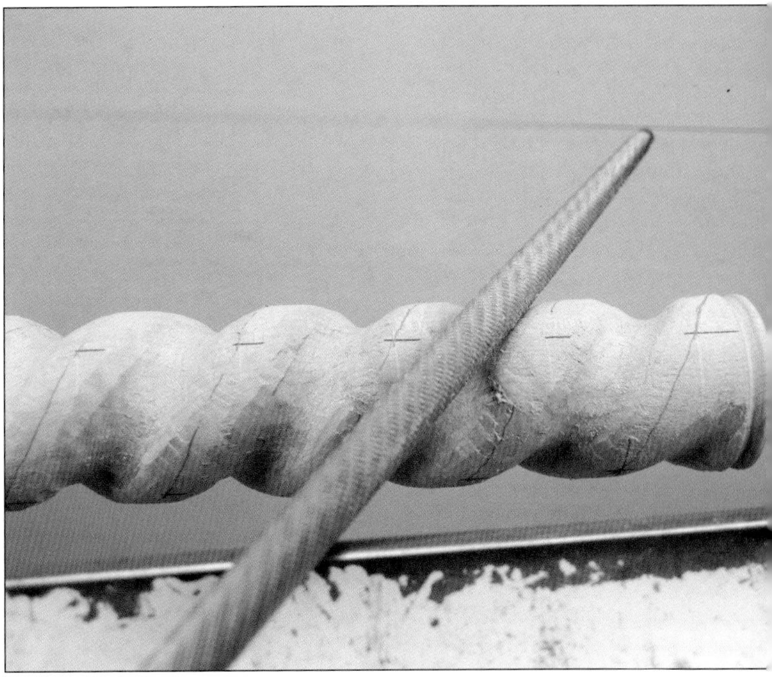

Remember to file perpendicularly as well as angularly, touching both right and left sides of the bines as the piece is hand-rotated.

Sanding is the next step and a good flexible abrasive that can be twisted into ropes is most helpful (Klingspor 1 inch yellow rolls 80, 100, 120, 150, 180, 220, 320, and 400 grits or Vitex pliable tearable sheets 80, 120, 150, 240, and 320 grits torn in 1/2 inch or 1/4 inch wide pieces). Sometimes a tapered sanding stick wrapped with various grits of sandpaper is helpful for larger twists. Once again, don't sand with the lathe on and don't use steel wool with the lathe running. It can catch and cause thinner pieces to snap in half!

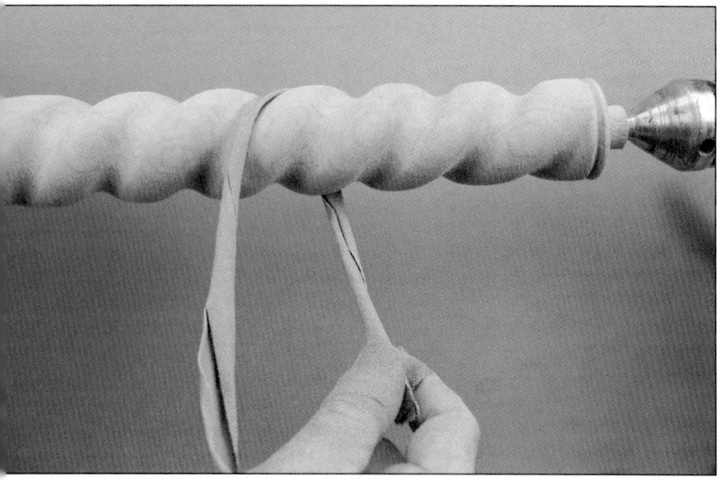

Progressive grits twisted into ropes are utilized to hand-sand the coves and bines to a smooth surface ready for your finish of choice.

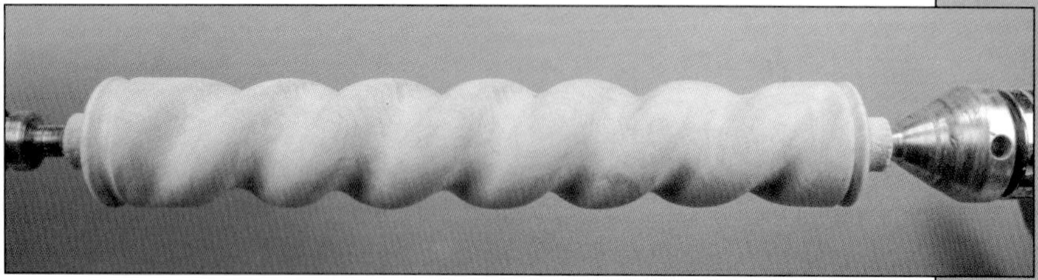

I prefer a satin finish, wipe-on polyurethane as it is environmentally safe, reasonably priced, stable, water resistant, easy to care for, and doesn't give a plastic appearance to the wood like gloss finishes do. Lacquers may become marked by perspiration from the hands. Oils tend to dry out with time but can be reapplied.

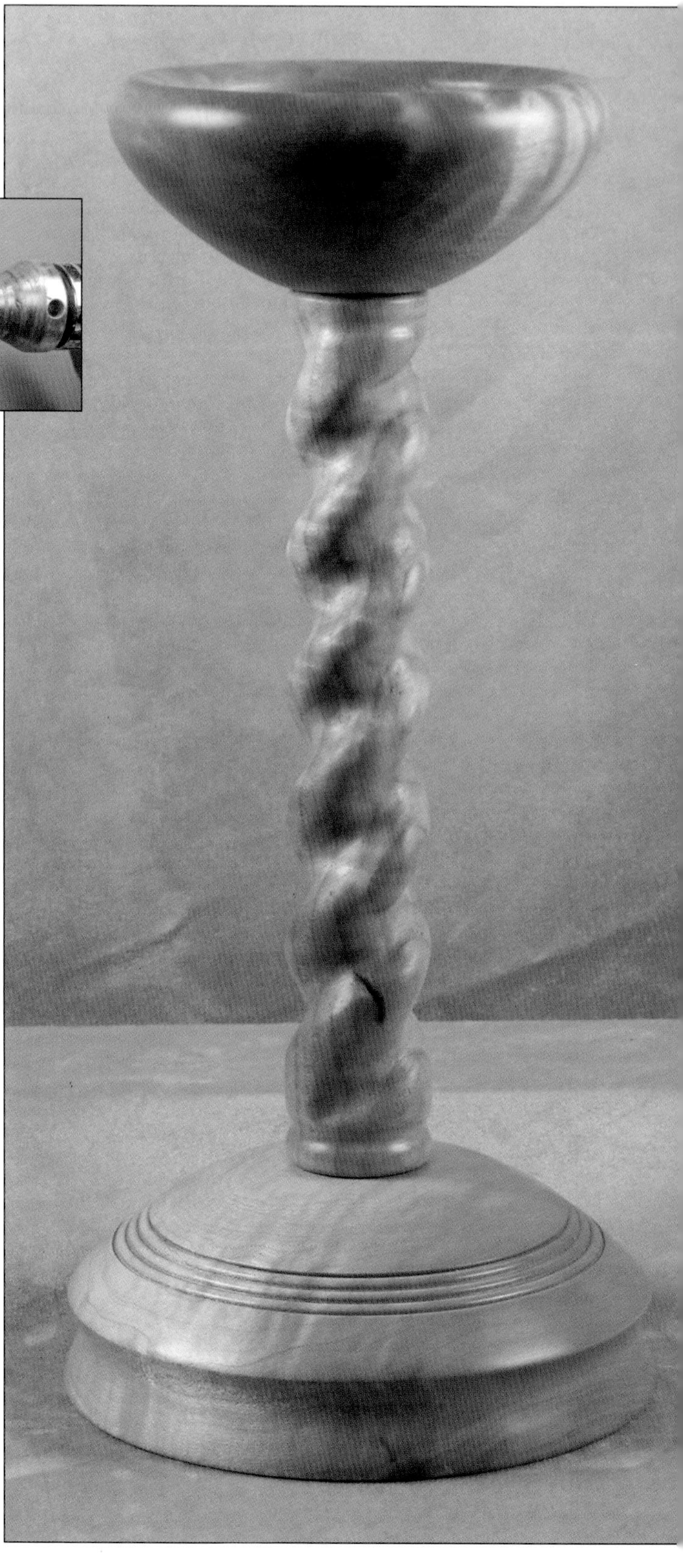

After the piece dries the dowels may be glued into turned bottom and top pieces for the finished product.

Single Twists

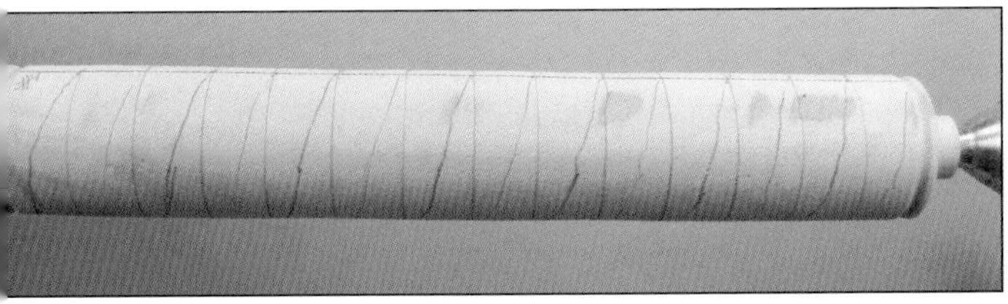

A single twist is fashioned similarly to the double, only 2 start lines are utilized. After turning the stock to a cylinder, turning 3/4 inch dowels or spigots 1/2 inch in length, coves and beads at either end, mark 2 start lines at 24 and 48 with the index. Mark 3 pitch lines 3 inches apart from the headstock cove, divide them in half (1-1/2 inches), and divide those in half again (3/4 inches) giving 14 segments. For a left-handed twist draw a baby blue line from the lower left hand corner to the upper right hand corner of the first rectangle and follow it all the way around to the tailstock end. Do the same for the other rectangle using the fluorescent pink marker. These are the bine and cut lines.

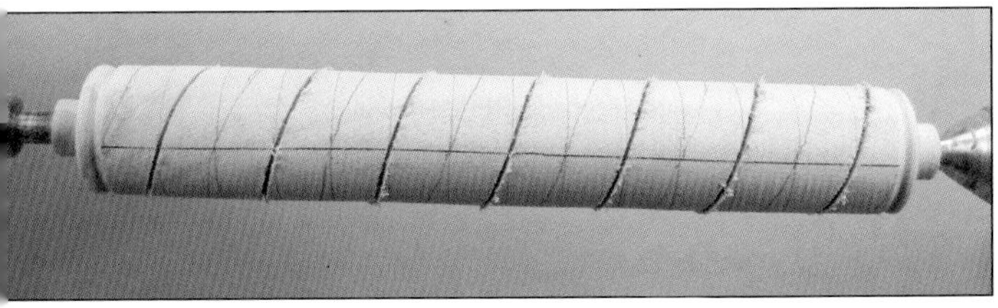

Use the dovetail saw to cut a kerf 1/4 inch deep all the way around to the tailstock end.

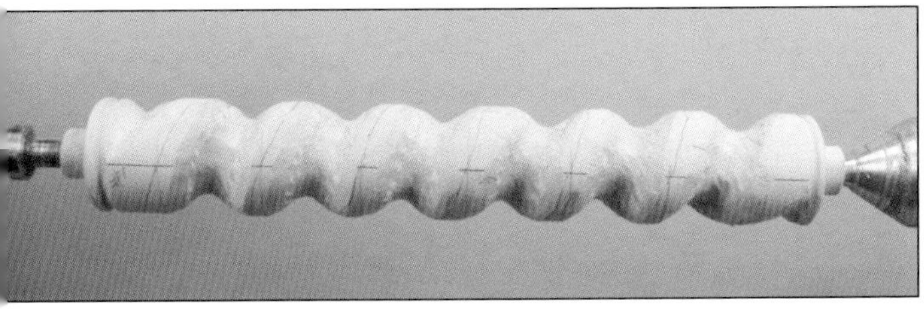

As before use the large round microplane to cut the cove, locking the spindle and working each parallel cove to the tailstock. Unlock the spindle, hand-rotate the cylinder and continue rasping until a smooth cove is fashioned. Use the shoulder or hobby plane to round over the bines. Go through the various files to smooth the wood then sand using the abrasives as was done for the double barley twist.

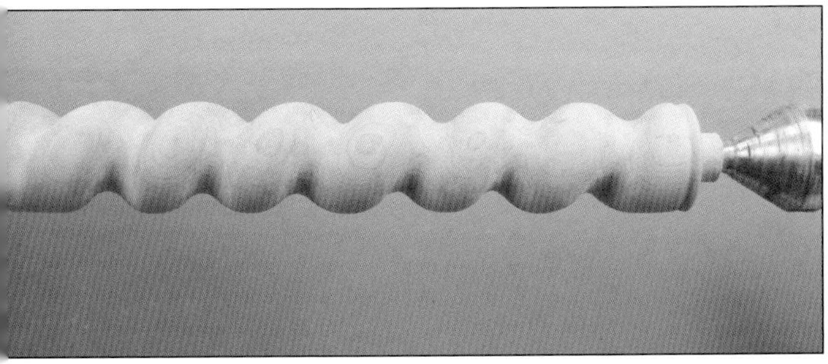

A single twist is fashioned. I really don't care for the single and only use it in special circumstances where its presence is oft times subdued by other more elaborate twists and/or decorations. The only good looking single twist in my estimation is a wooden thread.

Triple Twists

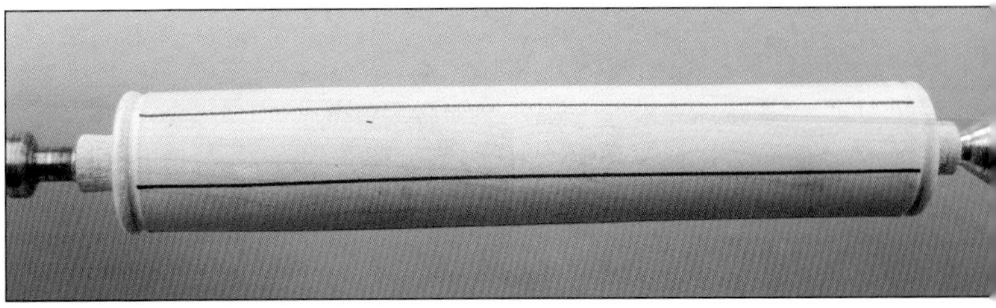

Triple twists are again similar to doubles, except that 6 start lines at 8, 16, 24, 32, 40, and 48 are drawn.

Mark pitch lines every 3/4 inches starting at the tailstock end.

Mark a #1 in a rectangle at the tailstock end for the right handed twist then rotate the cylinder skipping a rectangle to mark #2. Again rotate skipping a rectangle and mark #3. In each rectangle marked draw a baby blue line from the lower right hand corner to the upper left hand corner, continuing into the next diagonally adjacent rectangle until the bottom or headstock end is reached. Do the same for rectangles #2 and #3. In the unmarked rectangles draw a fluorescent pink line from the lower right hand corner to the upper left hand corner, continuing into the next diagonally adjacent rectangle until the bottom or headstock end is reached. Do the same for the remaining 2 rectangles.

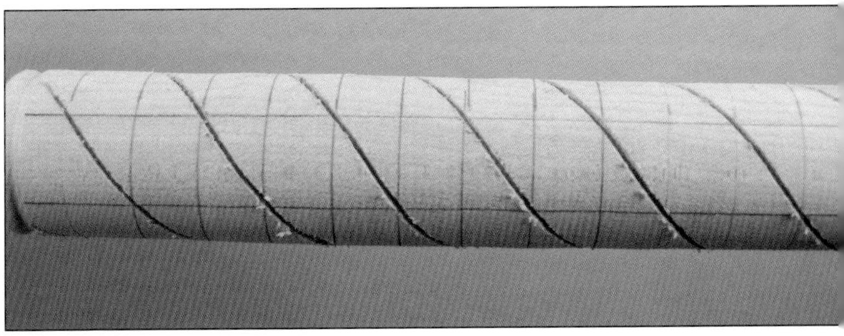

With the dove tail saw cut a 1/4 inch deep kerf on each fluorescent pink cut line from top to bottom. With the large microplane start to rasp a shallow cove just down to the bottom of the kerf.

Next go to a medium microplane to finish the coves.

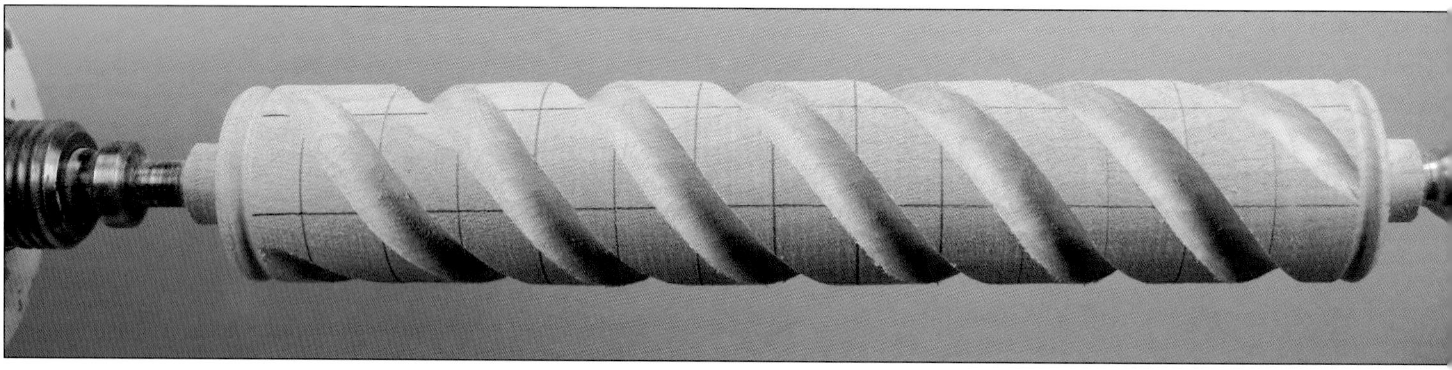

The coves are narrower than those of single or double twists. Remember as you increase the number of twists the coves and bines become narrower—the exception is a wooden thread.

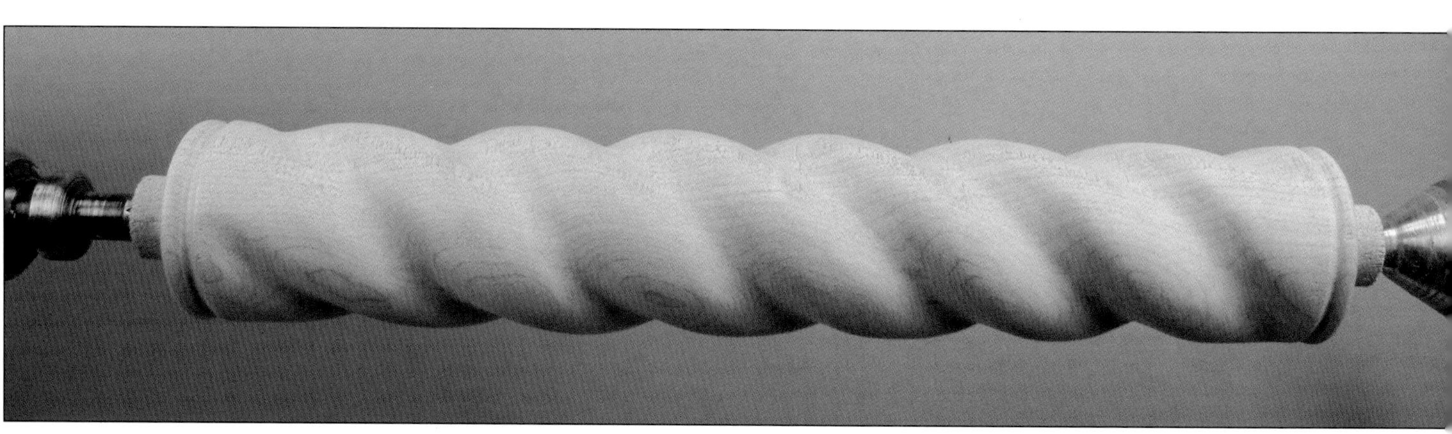

Continue finishing by using the hobby plane, files, and sanding ropes. For left-handed twists start at the headstock end with the measurements and the start of bine and cut lines.

Quadruple Twists
Twist Variations

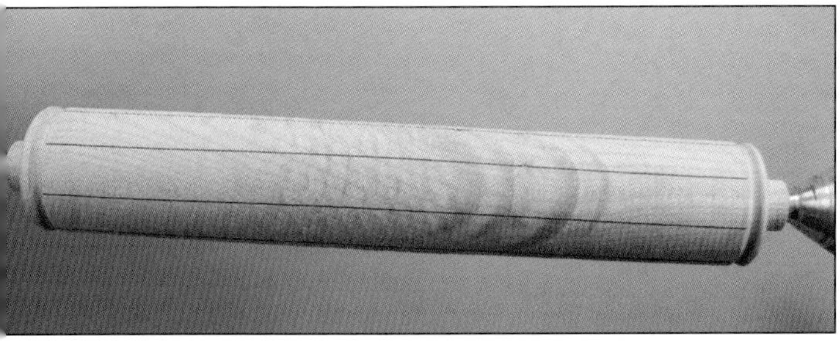

For quadruple twists, the layout has 8 start lines at 6, 12, 18, 24, 30, 36, 42, and 48.

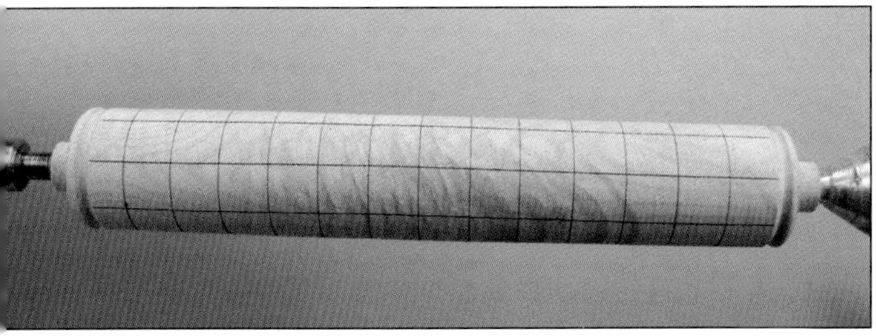

The pitch lines are drawn the same as for the double or triple, that is, every 3 inches from the tailstock cove and divided in half two times giving 14 segments longitudinally and 8 rectangles circumferentially. Mark every other rectangle at the tailstock #1, #2, #3, and #4.

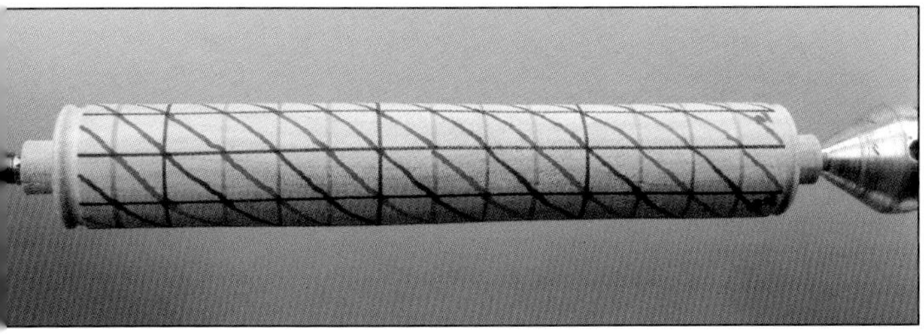

Draw diagonal baby blue lines from right to left around to the bottom or headstock end. In the unnumbered rectangles draw fluorescent pink lines to the bottom. You should have 4 baby blue and 4 fluorescent pink lines.

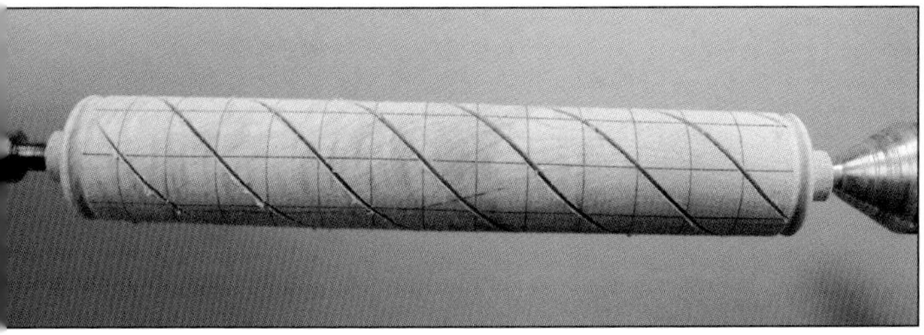

Next cut with the dovetail saw kerfs on the fluorescent pink lines.

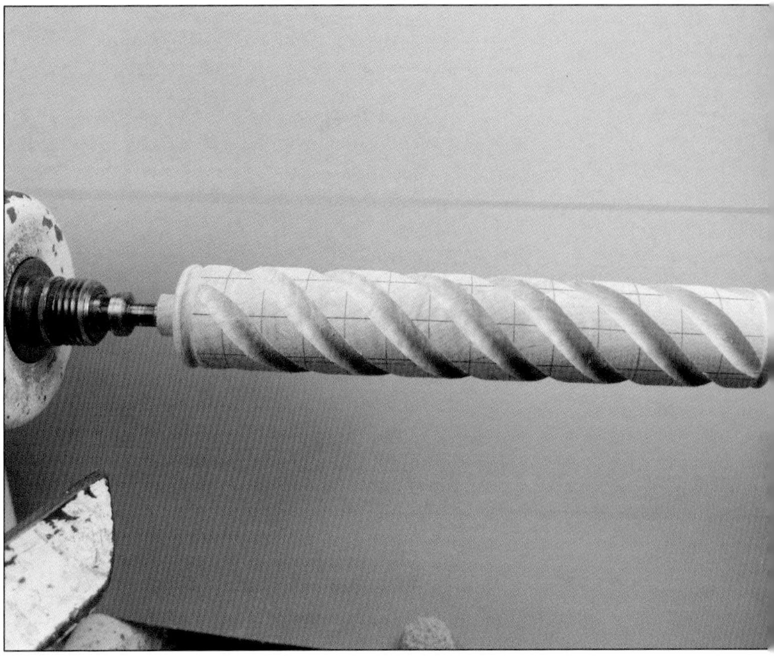

Be careful not to cut too deeply with the large round microplane. After shallow cuts go to the medium microplane since both bines and coves are narrow. Use the small hobby plane to round over the bines, then coarse to fine files. Sand the coves and bines with graduated sanding rope grits.

The finished right-handed quadruple twist is ready to apply the wipe-on polyurethane.

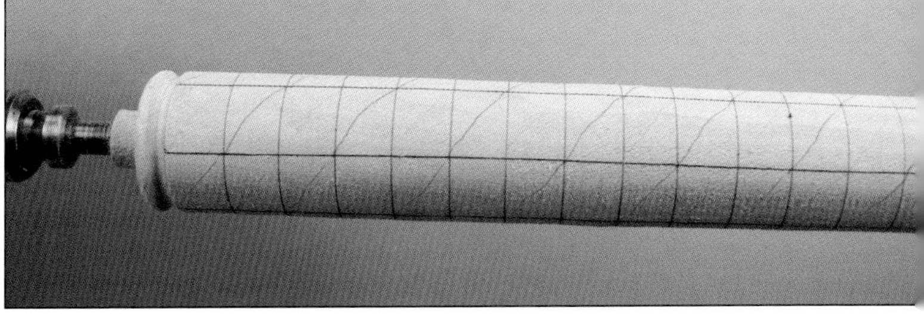

Coves broadened and bines cut sharp instead of rounded over produce twists that look like ribbons. If the layout is accomplished as for the standard left-handed triple twist and coves are cut deeply with the large, round microplane making perpendicular cuts as well as angular cuts, the finished sanded look of twisted ribbons is obtained.

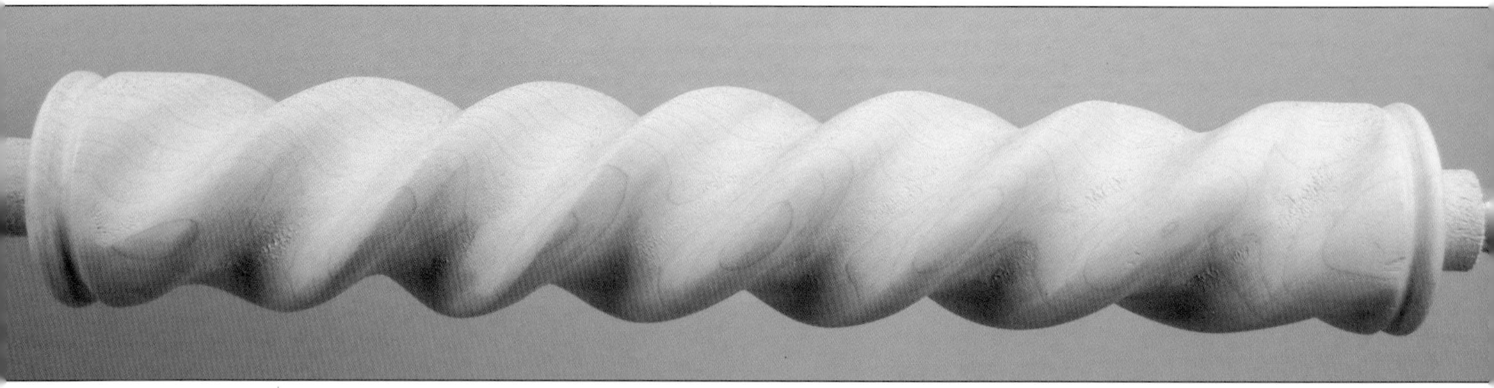

The finished ribbon twist is ready for polyurethane application.

If one cuts more of a "V" groove instead of a cove the appearance is that of twisted ropes. Doing a layout as we had for a right-handed quadruple twist, making shallow saw kerf cuts, and using the small microplane will give a good start to the quadruple rope twist. Remember to be gentle with the small microplane as it is rather fragile and fractures easily after heating with use—I always break several whenever using them.

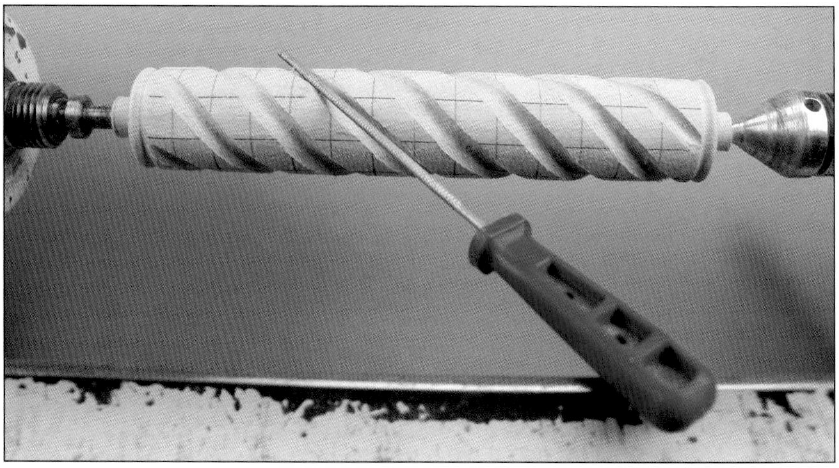

Use the 3/16 inch rasp at the bottom of the small cove, then go to the 1/8 inch rasp. (If you have difficulty acquiring round rasps try using round rifflers of the same diameter.)

Round over the bines with the small hobby or shoulder plane.

Sand with Vitex ropes. I find using the Klingspor rolls works best for sanding larger twists and Vitex best for narrow, fine, or thin open twists.

The completed quadruple rope twist has a pleasing appearance. You may wish to change the diameter of your work piece or the grade of your pitch to obtain various artistic effects. Remember twists are only limited by your imagination.

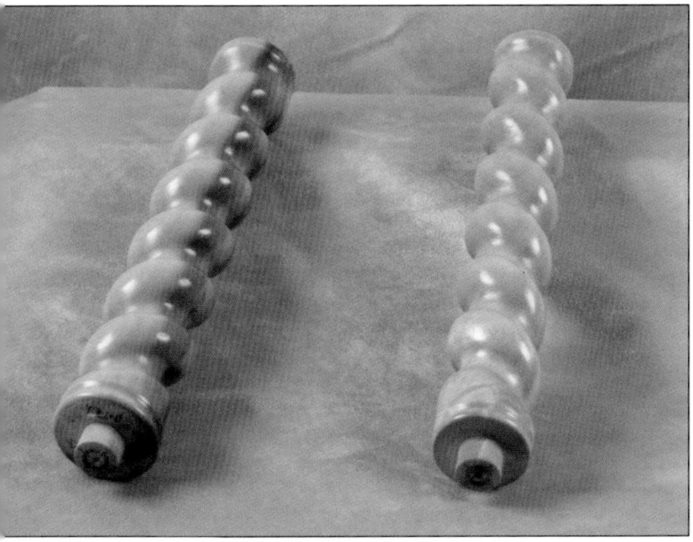

A finished pair of right- and left-handed single twists with wipe-on polyurethane finish.

A collection of double barley twists. At the far left is a left-handed twist next to a right-handed twist. Note, on the right-handed twist, what unpleasing appearances are had whenever the bines are left flat instead of rounded over. The third twist from the left has a pitch of 4-1/2 inches instead of 3. The far right double barley twist (right-handed) has a pitch of 2 inches. Note the various effects by just changing the pitch.

The far left, right-handed triple twist is contrasted with the left-handed triple ribbon twist next to it. The quadruple right-handed twist (third from left) is contrasted with the quadruple right-handed rope twist (far right).

A tapered left-handed triple twisted walking stick in cherry.

CHAPTER 2

OPEN TWISTS AND OPEN TWIST VARIANTS

In the last chapter basic spiral turning and its application were discussed at length. In this chapter the techniques will be applied to open twists and open twist variants. The praxis is very similar to closed twists, with only a few added steps to create an artistic appearance.

In spite of open twists being more decorative, denser timbers, such as exotics or closed-grain domestic hardwoods, must be used. One is essentially fashioning a wooden spring and consequently much support is lost. Soft woods are too pliable resulting in springy non-supportive open twists that have the propensity to fracture under the stress of production (mircroplaning, rasping, and most importantly, sanding).

Mango Candlesticks

The timber selected for the first project is mango, an easily worked, semi-dense tropical wood with interesting chromaticity. Since the design will be a pair of right- and left-handed candlesticks, two pieces of 2 by 2 by 9 inch stock are utilized.

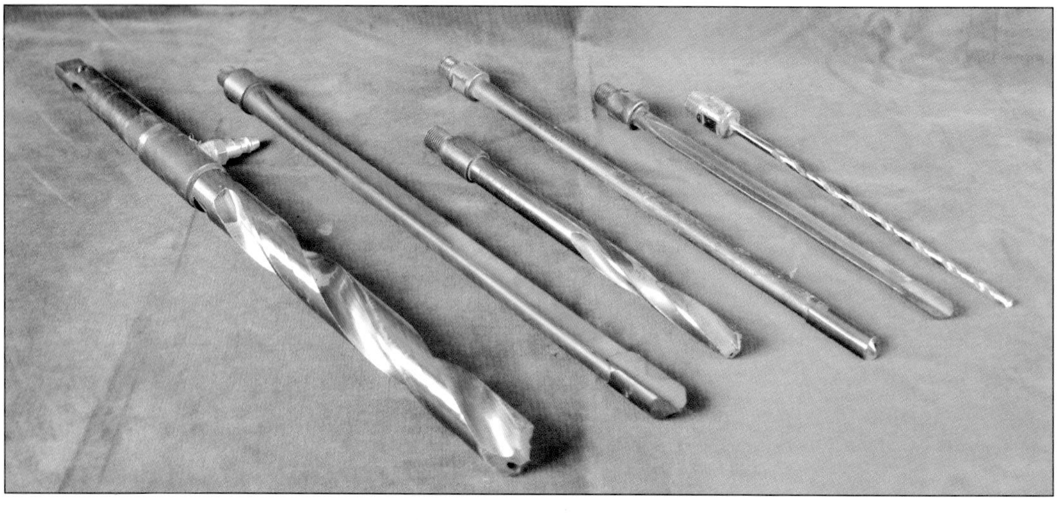

To drill holes in stock on the lathe, any long stable drill bit through the headstock or in a Jacob's chuck at the tailstock may be used, but surplus aircraft drill bits are employed for best results.

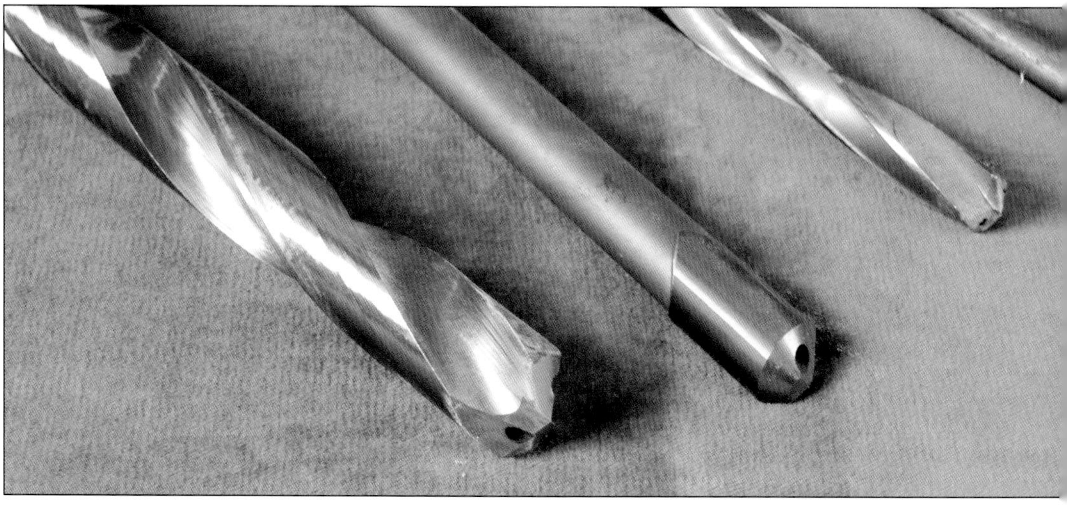

The bits were originally used on metal, with oil pumped through their lumens as a lubricant and cooling agent.

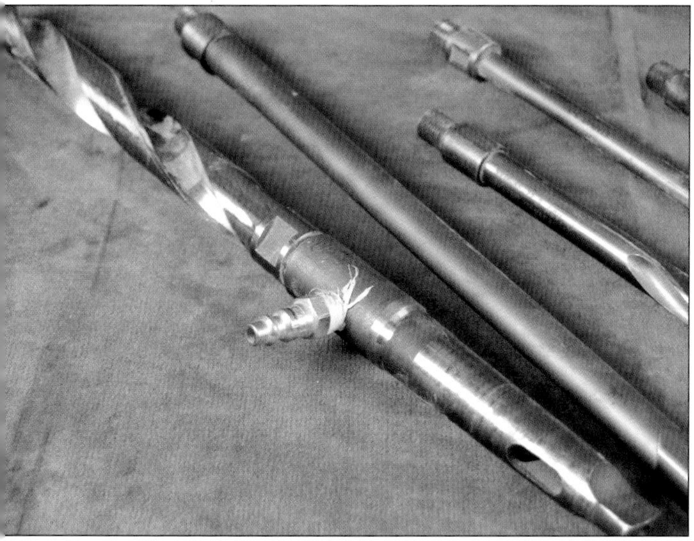

A number three Morse taper (Oneway tailstock) and compressed air hose fitting were fashioned on a metal blank tapped to fit the screw-in bits. The compressed air helps remove shavings and cool the bore hole as well as the drill bit.
Various sizes of bits from 3/16 inches to 1 inch may be employed. For the 2 by 2 inch stock a 1/2 inch or 5/8 inch bit is used, depending on how thick the bines will be. The larger diameter of the hole, the thinner the bines will be.

After marking the centers at either end mount the stock in a good self-centering 4-jaw chuck with a large enough center opening so the particular size drill bit being used will not foul on the chuck's jaws. Turn a cylindrical area at the tailstock end to allow utilization of a spindle steady. There are many commercially available spindle steadies, but many turners have fashioned their own which work just as well.

Drill a pilot hole 1/2 inch deep and 1/2 inch in diameter at the tailstock using a Jacob's chuck and short drill bit then switch to the compressed air drill bit. One must be extremely careful drilling advancing a millimeter per turn at 200 to 300 rpms. A very firm grip with gloved hand on the compressed air fitting, as well as an accessible on-off switch must be utilized. The remote stop button can easily be hit with a knee if the drill bit binds and the air hose begins to wrap around the bit. On-off floor switches could also be employed but floor switches tend to become lost in shavings and dust, creating another shop hazard.

After the 7 inch deep hole is bored remount the stock between centers, true both ends, and true-up the tailstock cylindrical area. The stock is reversed, mounted in the 1-1/2 inch O'Donnell jaws with the tailstock end (previously the headstock end) turned true so that the spindle steady may be used again.

Using a tapered candle cup drill bit, drill a 7/8 inch deep tapered hole.

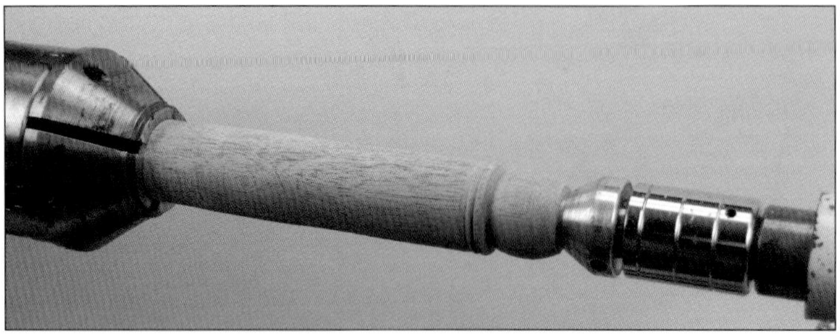

Replace the Jacob's chuck with a live center and turn the complete cylinder turning a candle cup and several beads at the tailstock end. It may seem rather repetitious with remounting and turning, but one must remember that each time a long drill bit is employed a perfect bore hole is never made. No matter what size bit is used the bit will always follow the path of least resistance in the wood, flexing from center to create a bore hole that is not exactly centered. The thinner and longer the bit the greater the deviation. By remounting and turning every time a new hole is drilled (using the newly bored hole as the center) the more likely the bored center hole will actually be in the center but the thinner the piece becomes.
The cylinder is remounted again using a 7/8 inch diameter collet chuck and the live center. Several beads and a cove turned at the tailstock leaves about 6 inches of material for twists on the now 1-3/4 inch diameter cylinder. As was done in chapter 1, start lines at 12, 24, 36, and 48 (48 point index) and pitch lines every 3 inches from the headstock cove, divided in half twice, give the beginning layout for a left-handed double barley twist. For the right-handed double barley one would start the layout from the tailstock end.

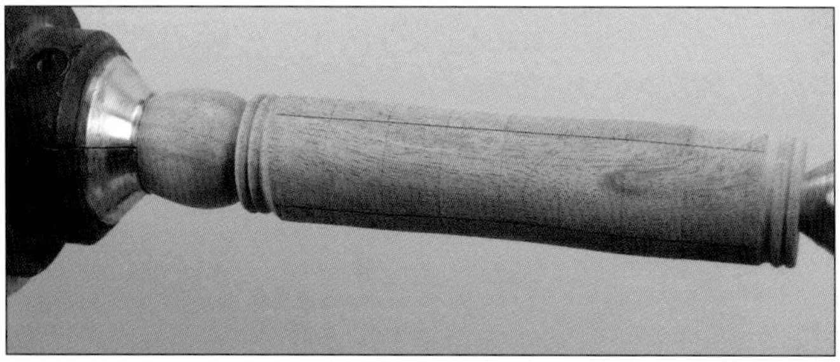

At the headstock end mark one rectangle #1, skip a rectangle and mark #2. Draw a baby blue diagonal in rectangle #1 from the lower left hand corner to the upper right hand corner following into the adjacent rectangle until the tailstock end is reached. Do the same for rectangle #2. In the other rectangles draw fluorescent pink lines so that the layout is complete.

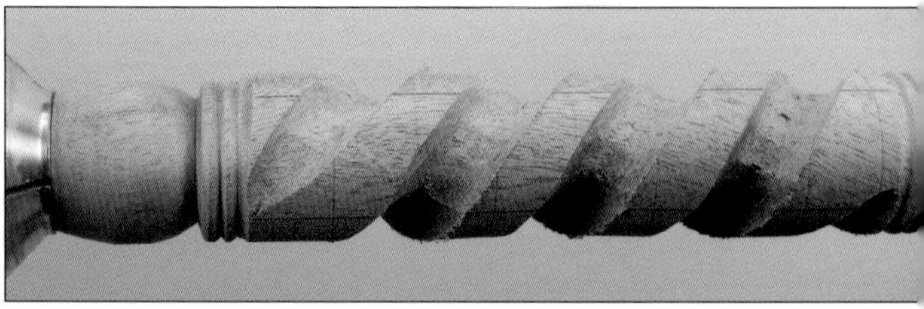

Use the dowel or dovetail saw to cut guide grooves (kerfs) about 1/2 inch deep along the pink fluorescent cut lines. Rasping with the large microplane remove material carefully without breaking through to the lumen.

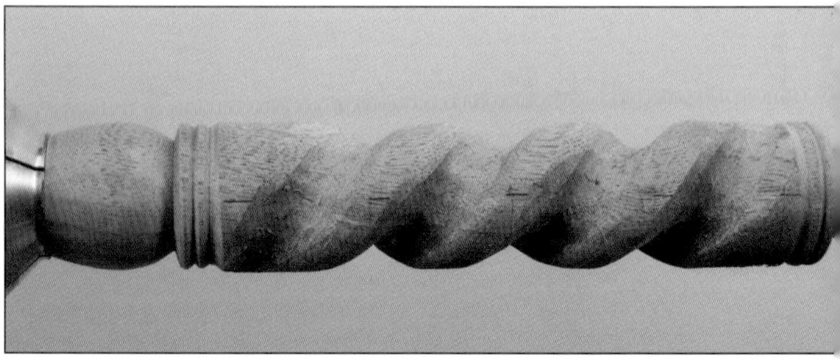

When enough material is removed to give a hint of breakthrough, while maintaining structural integrity, use the hobby plane or shoulder plane to round over the bines before continue rasping with the microplane.

After breakthrough utilize coarse to fine files to round over the undersides of the bines being careful not to fracture them.

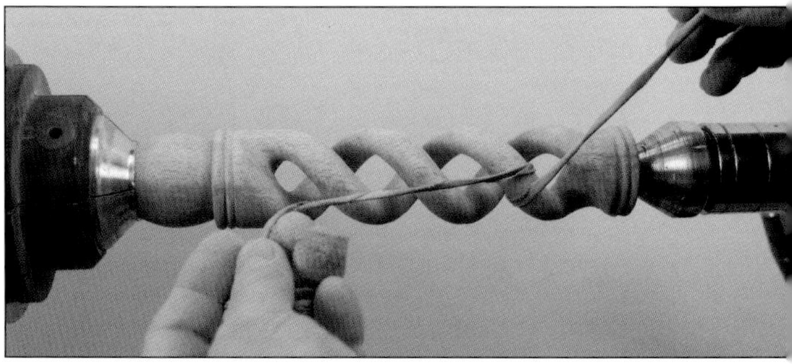

Sand all surfaces of the bines with Vitex sanding ropes in 80, 120, 150, 240, and 320 grits to give a smooth finish. Next glue the twist on to a turned base with a 1/2 inch turned dowel to fit the candlestick's bored hole or turn the dowel on the base. (If turning a dowel use the same wood instead of commercially available dowels).

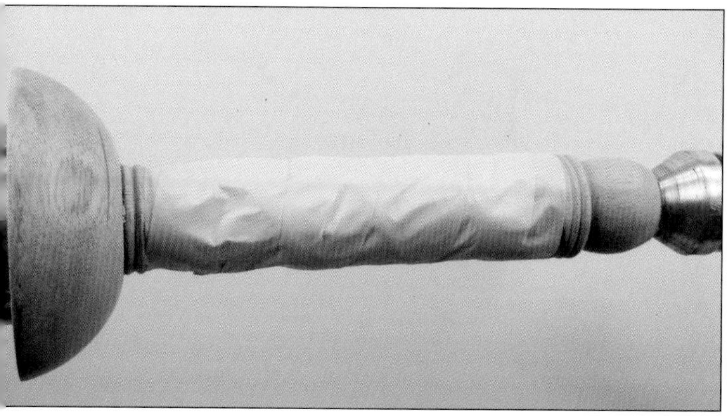

For further sanding of the cup, beads, and coves, wrap the twist with masking tape to prevent fracture from centrifugal force while turning.

The finished product is ready for wipe-on polyurethane.

Right- and left-handed double barley open twists make a handsome pair when completed.

Ebony Candlesticks

Another interesting open twist project is a pair of ebony candlesticks for pillars or tapers. A 2 by 2 by 8 inch stock mounted in a self-centering 4-jaw chuck is accomplished in the same fashion as for the mango candlesticks. After the center hole is drilled the piece is remounted in the O'Donnell jaws and the live center tailstock is brought up. When turning ebony one must be very cautious of the fine irritating dust, a most insalubrious substance, equalled or surpassed only by the toxicity of cocobolo dust, which bothers the eyes as well as the lungs. An Airmate respirator and face shielded helmet would be a welcomed appliance.

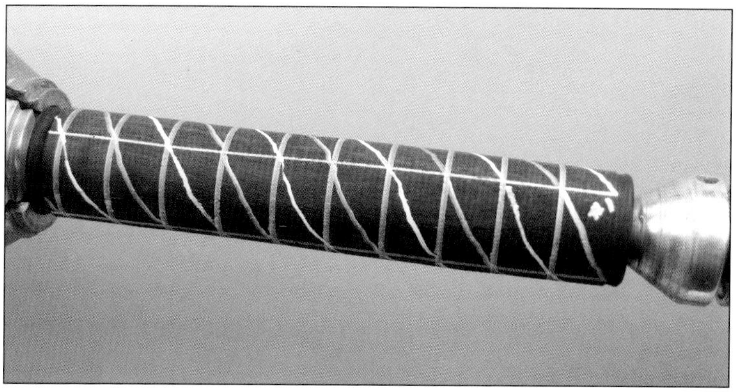

Marking the ebony presents another problem as most lines can't be seen. A silver Sharpie and white-out pen are most helpful for the layout.

Make the dovetail saw cuts.

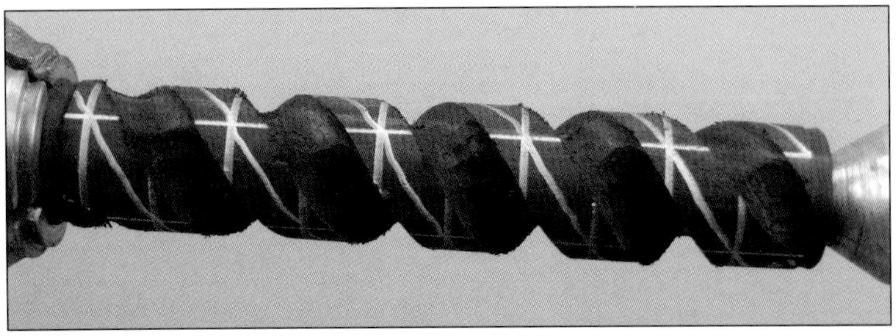

Use the large microplane, rasping to the point of breakthrough.

Use the small hobby plane to round over the bines.

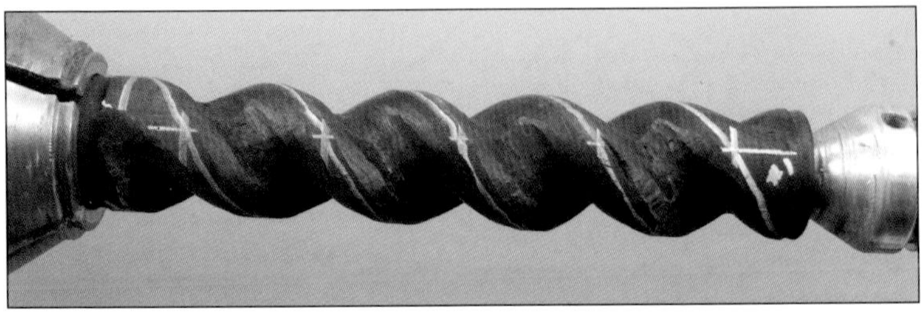

Next use the medium microplane to breakthrough.

Much care must be taken here as ebony fractures easily due to lack of interlocking fibers. It also readily cracks due to the heat produced by either turning or sanding.

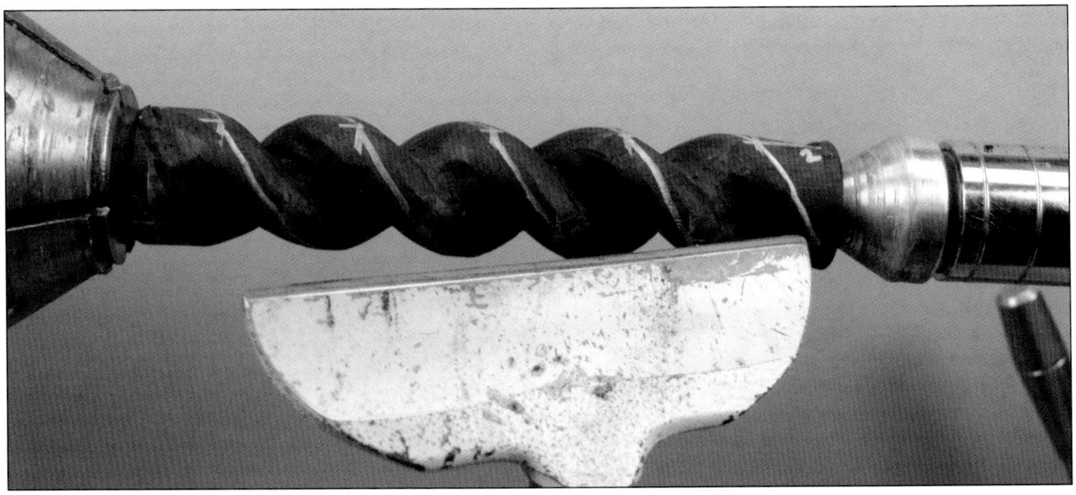

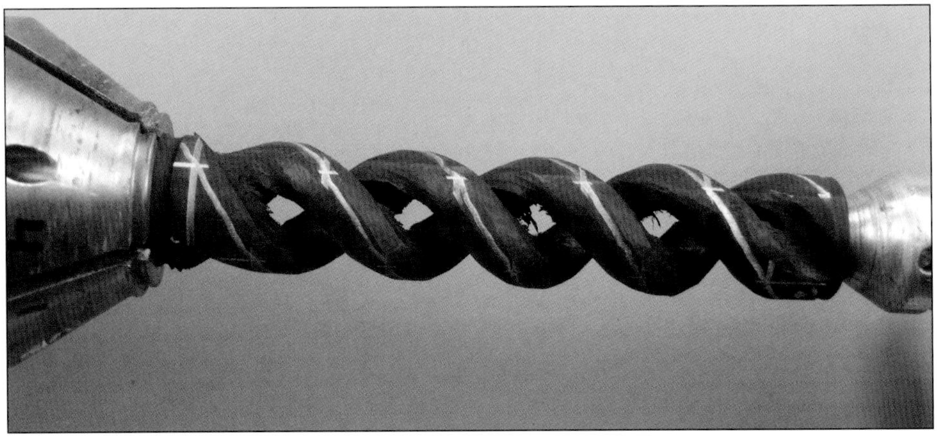

The medium and small microplanes also have the propensity to break upon use. Plan on at least 3 for each open twist made in such hard wood.

Great care must be exercised in rasping and filing the undersides of the bines as fracture frequently happens.

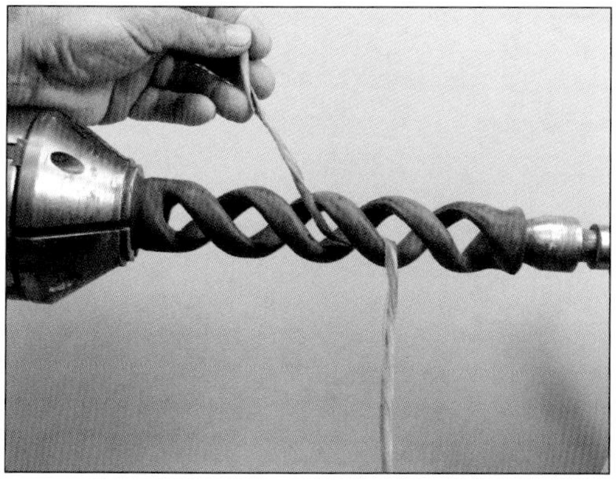

Vigorous sanding with Vitex ropes cannot be done, so a gentile touch is necessary to create a fine finished twist.

The fruits of careful sanding are obvious.

After turning bases, tops and applying a finish, a lovely pair of ebony candlesticks can be created.

Triple Open Twists

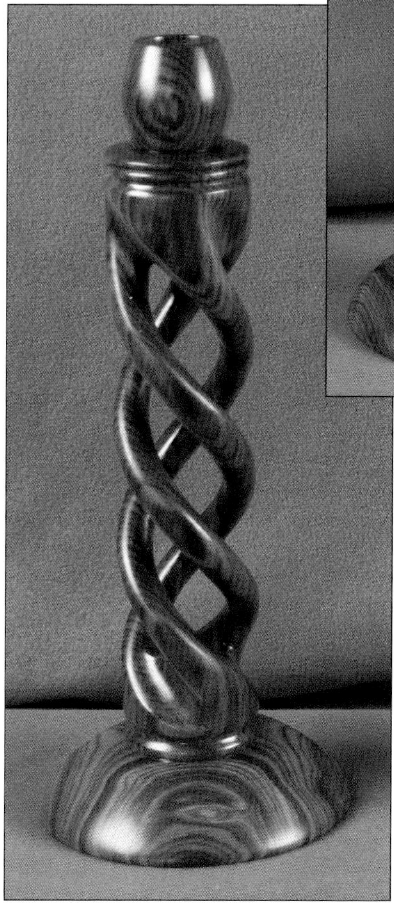

As with the double, a triple open twist with nicely rounded bines may be crafted by creating larger bore holes. This is accomplished by using a 1 inch diameter aircraft drill bit on a 2 by 2 by 10 inch long piece of an exotic such as kingwood. Care must be taken as the large drill bit has a tendency to bind and grab. One must be proficient in the quick knee-off button operation.

After bore holes and candle cups are drilled, beads and coves turned, the triple twist layout may be drawn. With a 48 point index start lines are drawn at 8, 16, 24, 32, 40, and 48. Pitch lines are drawn every 3-1/2 inches and divided in half twice. Bine and cut lines are drawn in. The same procedure as for the open double is carried out with sanding ropes and a wipe-on polyurethane finish to give a delightful pair of open triple twist sticks. Note the triple has only one complete revolution as opposed to two for the double.

Quadruple Open Twists

Quadruple twists are produced similarly, except start lines are drawn at 6, 12, 18, 24, 30, 36, 42, and 48 (48 point index). The pitch may be lengthened slightly to give a different effect. Smaller microplanes need to be used so that the bines and spacings are the same diameters. It will require a small fortune in medium and small microplanes as they frequently fracture on dense exotic timbers; nevertheless, just like in figure skating a quadruple twist is most impressive.

Open Twist Variants

An impressive effect and stable support of weaker timbers can be obtained by turning contrasting dowels to glue into the bored holes made for open twists. Combinations such as ebony or blackwood in cherry or holly, yellow heart in cocobolo, red heart or walnut in maple, holly in ebony or cocobolo, give delightful heterogeneities.

The drilling must be accomplished without much deviation so that an off-centered variant is not formed. If a long twist—drilling from either end—is desired, care must be taken to have a straight bore hole, otherwise an unsightly gap will occur destroying the integrity of the open twist variant. It is also suggested to allow the glue, whether it is yellow glue or cyanoacrylate, to dry for at least 24 hours before turning the open twist variant.

Another easy project is once again a candlestick. After the bore hole is drilled, dowel glued into place and allowed to dry, the stock is trued-up and mounted in the collet chuck.

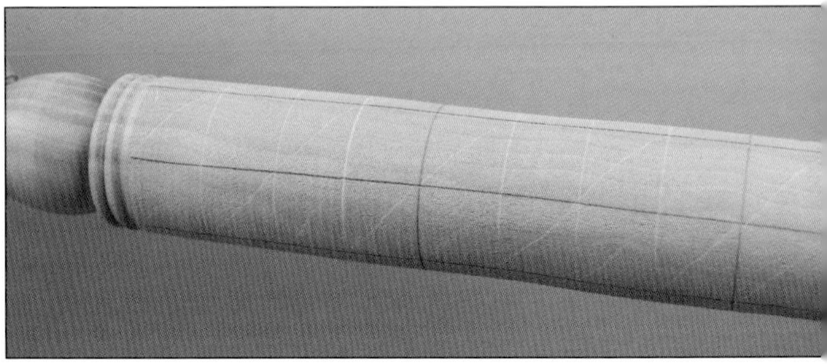

A layout for left-handed twist is accomplished.

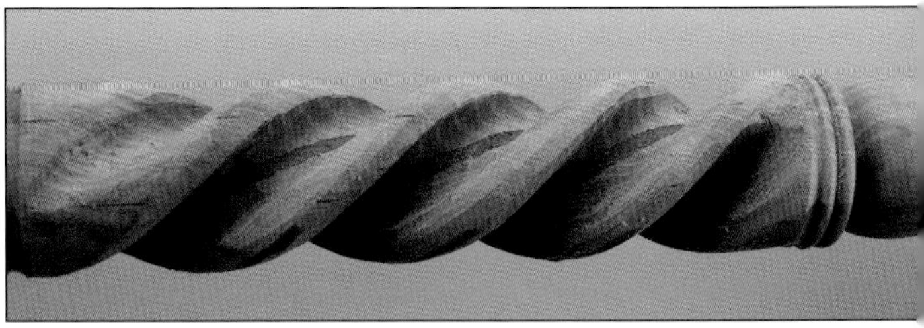

The triple twist is carved using only the large microplane giving a ribbon-type twist and exposing the red heart core beneath.

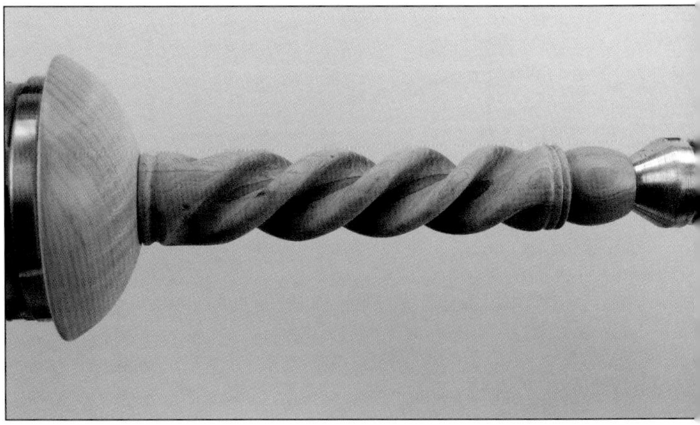

Finish filing, sanding, and gluing on a base to create an open twist variant.

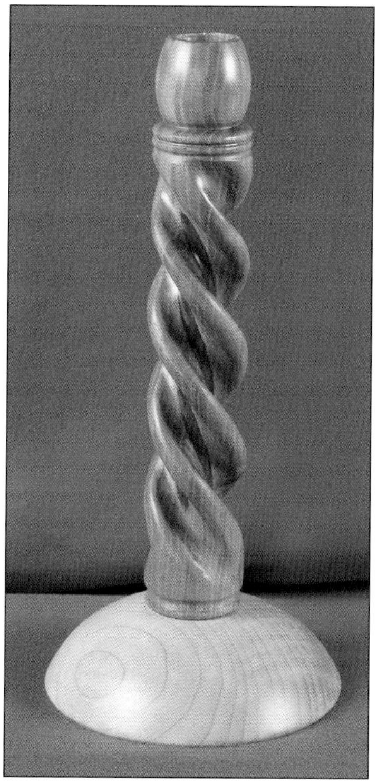

The triple ribbon left handed open twist variant finishes well with wipe-on polyurethane.

Between centers rough out the blank. A long tool rest utilizing 2 banjos is most helpful. This prevents irregularities as well as accidents from moving a shorter tool rest back and forth.

Walking sticks lend themselves to open twist variants. First the 1-3/4 by 1-3/4 by 36 inch long walking stick blank needs a cylindrical area turned at the tailstock end to accommodate the spindle steady. Next drill a 3/4 inch, 12 inch deep hole, drilling a pilot hole first.

Using the spindle steady, fashion the correct taper of the walking stick. After the turned dowel is glued in and set aside to dry (about 24 hours), mark the layout for whichever type of twist is desired.

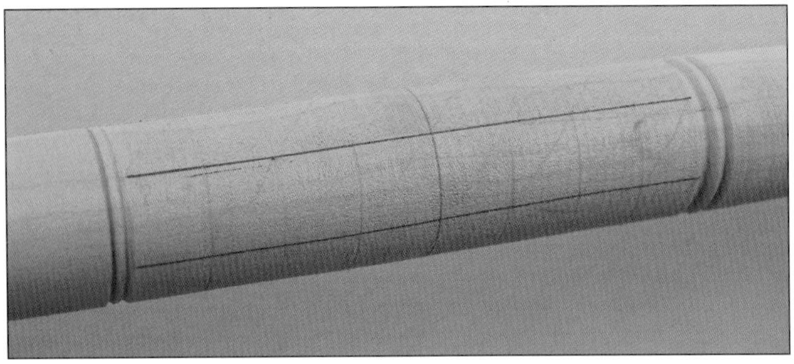

The photo shows the layout for a triple left-handed twist with beads at either end.

Proceed with rasping (large microplane), filing, sanding, and wipe-on polyurethane to give a lovely finished piece. One may note that the short twist near the top of the walking stick is very handy helping the elderly or infirmed to get up from a seated position. Instead of the hand sliding down, a very clutchable area is presented.

Another finished walking stick with right-handed, double barley open twist variant of cocobolo and yellow heart is displayed in the close-up.

If you ever drill a bore hole that deviates off to one side, glue in the dowel, and turn a triple ribbon twist, the end product is not usable. It will look terrible with the dowel off center. This is a design opportunity. The only other procedure to salvage the piece is to place colored Inlace resins in the coves. This makes a rather interesting pattern and pleasing piece, but remember to wear a painter's respirator when using the resins as they are very toxic.

Display of three walking sticks, 2 cherry and 1 cocobolo.

CHAPTER 3

THIN, VERY THIN, AND EXTREMELY THIN TWISTS

In the last chapter how to fashion open and open twist variants was discussed and demonstrated. The techniques will be utilized to make thin, very thin, and extremely thin twists. Although all three types are more difficult to produce, diligence, patience, and the delicate hand of a superior surgeon will result in a most bodacious end product.

Thin Twists

A nifty twist for goblet stems is the thin twist. One must decide on how tall the goblet pair will be. About 14 inches presents an impressive pair, but most shelving spaces are around 12 inches high or less. That would require a stem length of 7-1/2 inches when allowances for the base and cup of the goblet are considered. The goblet can be made in one piece with a variety of twists applicable to present a handsome finished product. An open twist variant yields a more attractive stem, but the goblet can't be turned in one piece. There virtually is no way to drill a 3/16 inch diameter bore hole in stock that is 3 by 3 by 12 inches and keep it centered. The alternative is to make the goblet in pieces and carefully turn and fit the parts together with adequate gluing.

The first step is to choose correct timber for the pair. Ebony with holly cores looks quite nice but ebony is most difficult to work as noted in the previous chapter. Cocobolo with holly is also quite nice but cocobolo dust tends to be somewhat insalubrious. Holly with blackwood cores is delightful, easy to work, and finishes well. Pear wood is another easily workable, turnable, pleasant timber.

The stock selected is 1 by 1 by 7-1/2 inches mounted between centers. A cylindrical form to fit the spindle steady is turned at the tailstock end. The stock is then mounted in a 4-jaw self-centering chuck and the spindle steady. Next a pilot hole of 1/8 inch is drilled 1/4 inch deep using a Jacob's chuck in the tailstock. A 3/16 inch aircraft drill bit is substituted and connected to compressed air. Carefully the bit is advanced 1 mm per turn at 200 to 300 rpms. The compressed air cools the wood as well as the bit and forces out the shavings.

After the hole is drilled thorough inspection of the pear stock will display how far off center the bit has strayed. If one uses thinner stock to drill, oft times the bit will exit through the side of the piece. It may take 3 to 4 tries to get one drilled hole. As a consequence less wood is actually wasted using the 1 inch square stock. Next mount the stock between centers using a steb center (1/2 inch) in the headstock and a live center in the tailstock. Turn the dowel to a diameter of 1/2 inch.

If one desired a thinner stem then the dowel could be turned to 3/8 inches as noted in the displayed stems—1/2 inch on left, 3/8 inches on right.

Turn an 8-1/2 inch long 1/4 by 1/4 inch dowel of whatever contrasting wood is to be used. It is best to turn such stock at high rpms—about 4000—while supporting it with one's gloved fingers. The selection happens to be dry Honduran red heart, a good, stable, contrasting wood. The dowel should be turned to 3/16 inches (a good exercise to test adeptness with the skew). Check the fit of the drilled hole in the pear wood dowel. It should be quite tight but should slide on and off easily. The red heart dowel should extend about 1/2 to 3/4 inches beyond either end of the pear wood dowel so that the red heart dowel may be used in gluing the base and cup to the stem.

Glue in the dowel using flexible cyanoacrylate. The reason is much torque will be created with rasping and sanding; if a flexible glue is used it will be forgiving. After the piece dries (about 24 hours resting time) mount it between centers.

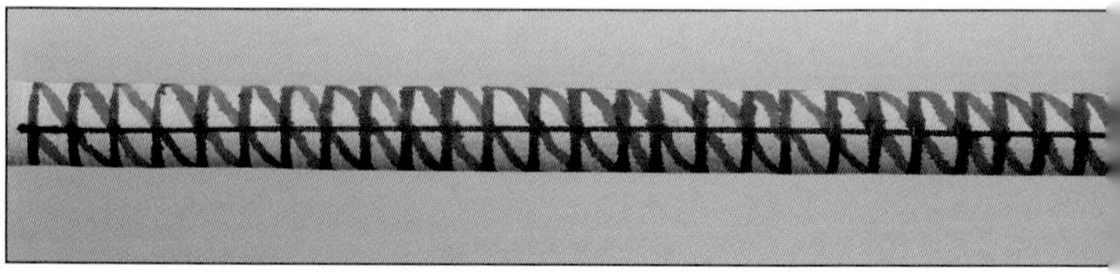

Mark out a double barley layout allowing 1/4 inch border at each end. This would require 4 start lines at 6, 12, 18, and 24 (24 point index). Mark pitch lines every 1 inch, divide in half twice giving circumferential lines every 1/4 inch. Draw from the tailstock end bine lines in baby blue and cut lines in fluorescent pink for the right handed twist.

Next, using the 3/16 inch diameter rasp, begin rasping along successive cut lines with the spindle locked and the stock supported by the free hand. Rotate the stock, lock the spindle, and repeat the rasping until all cut lines are completed. Be very careful to use a light, delicate touch. This is brain surgery.

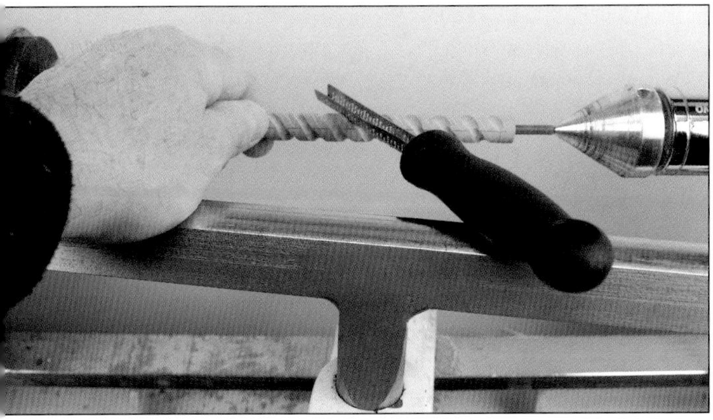

After the cove is as deep as the rasp's diameter (3/16 inch), use the small microplane to carefully round over the bines while the piece is supported with the free hand.

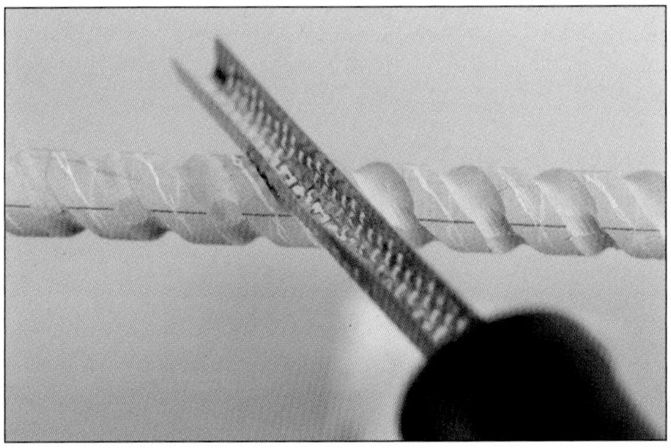

Use the microplane to round out the cove bottom but be careful not to remove too much material from the bines or fracture the edges (one side of the bine has no supporting fibers).

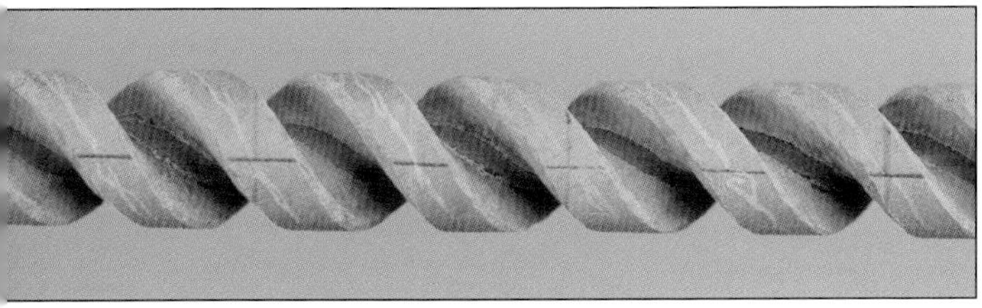

Go back to the 3/16 inch rasp to carefully rasp out to the red heart core. Next use thin coarse to fine files to finish the coves and bines.

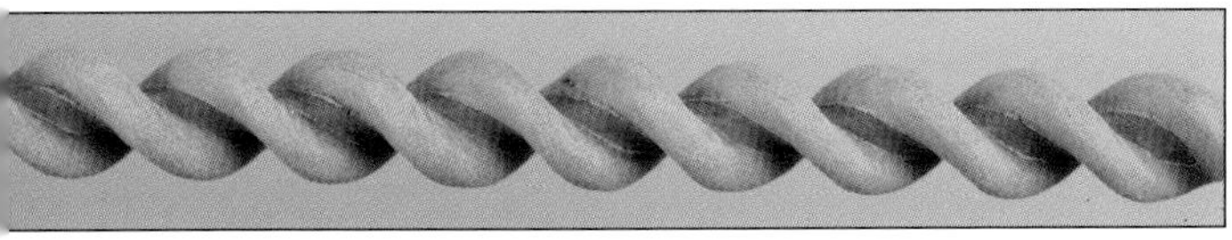

Proceed to sanding with Klingspor or Vitex ropes giving a nicely finished product. Make sure the ends are squared by using a small skew. Loosen the piece from the 4-jaw chuck and withdraw it about 3/8 inches to turn the square down to a 3/16 inch diameter dowel. This will be the dowel to glue into the base. After roughing out the 3 by 3 by 5 inch pear stock to a cylinder turn a tulip-shaped cup at the distal end of the stock mounted in the O'Donnell 2 inch jaws. Turn a small design to fit the diameter (1/2 inch) of the stem, sand the cup to completion, then part it off.

Turn the base with a design to fit the diameter of the stem then drill a 1/4 inch deep, 3/16 inch hole in the base. Sand to completeion before carefully parting it off.

Next mount the cup in either a turned wooden friction fit jam chuck or a deep 4-jaw custom chuck protecting the wood with material to prevent jaw marks. Drill a 1/4" inch deep 3/16 inch hole to fit the stem's dowel. Care must be taken initially when turning the cup to leave enough material in its base to account for the drilled hole while keeping the cup light, thin, and delicate.

The finished pair (left- and right-handed thin open twist variants) make handsome silver anniversary goblets for toasting.

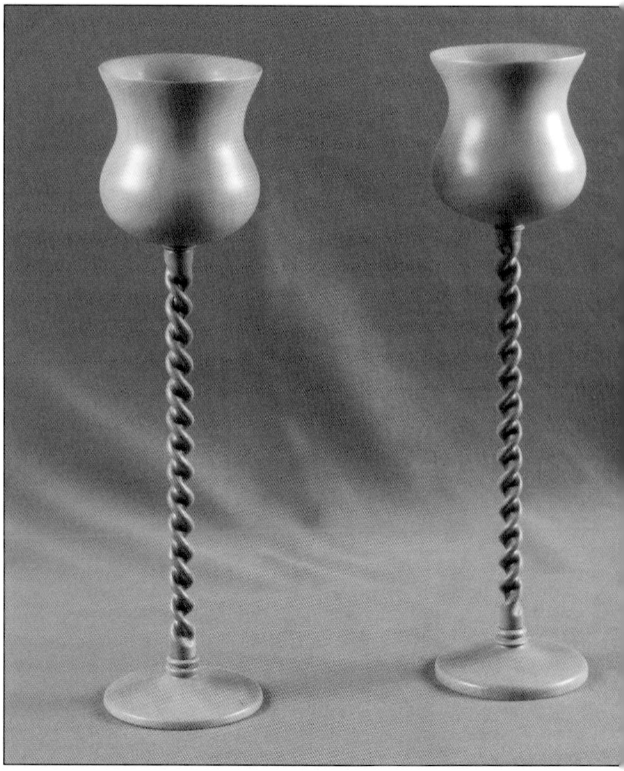

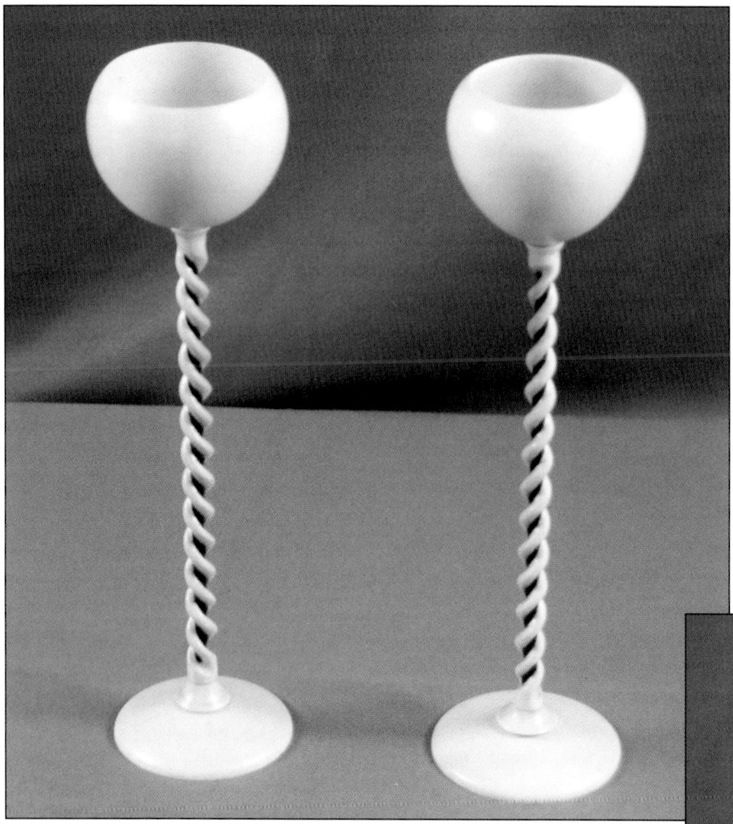

The pair of holly goblets is ideal for a wedding toast.

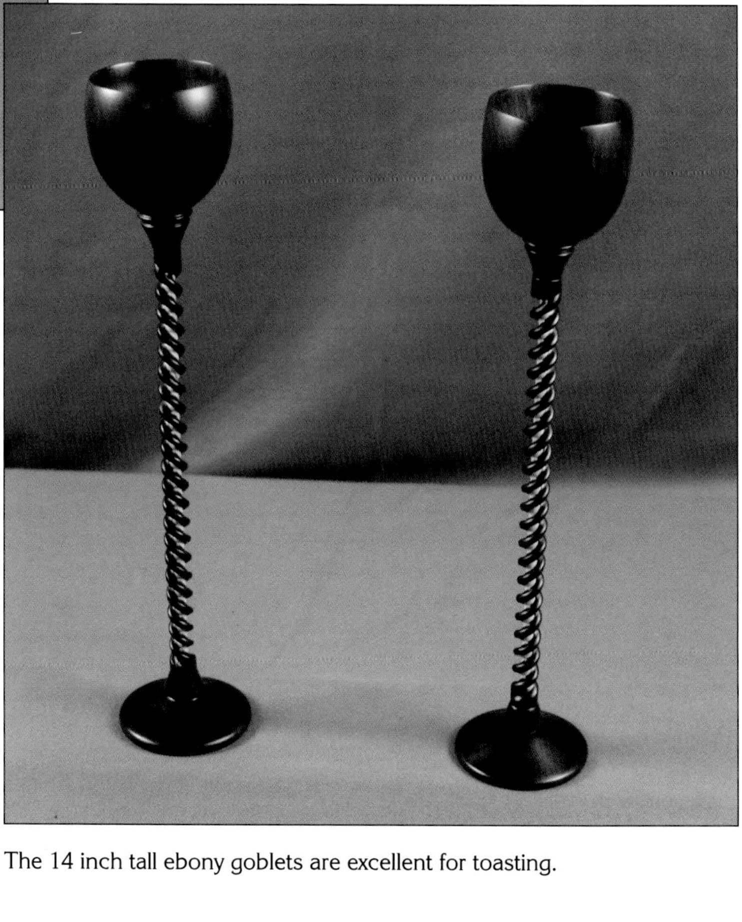

The 14 inch tall ebony goblets are excellent for toasting.

Cocobolo goblets are charming for any other type of toasting.

Very Thin Twists

Very thin twists are beautiful when completed but are one of the most frustrating, time consuming projects known to modern turners. Their production may drive a calm reserved gentleman (or lady) to manically homicidal irrationalities requiring potent sedation. The bines are so thin (about 3/16 to 1/4 inches) that they easily fracture if only gazed upon in an improper fashion.

Pink Ivory, with Yellow Heart and Blackwood

The timber chosen for the project is pink ivory, a most dense stone-like wood that turns and carves nicely. The stock is 1-3/4 by 1-3/4 by 8-1/2 inches. A bore hole 11/16 inches (15 mm) in diameter and 7 inches deep is carefully drilled using the spindle steady and aircraft drill bits. Using the same procedures previously described, great care must be taken because the drill bit has the propensity to catch, grab, and cause an instant catastrophe if not worked slowly and pedantically.

After the bore hole is drilled, a candle cup drilled and fashioned, the layout for a left handed triple twist is undertaken as described previously. It is best to use a new large round microplane as the pink ivory is very dense (.98) and hard as stone. The look desired is bines of about 3/8 inch diameter which would leave coves of 1/2 inch. When near breakthrough, round over the bines with the small hobby plane then proceed to breakthrough using the medium microplane.

To round over the undersides of bines use a Foredom (1/4 horse power) detailing tool with the small, easily hand-held pen and a tapered tungsten carbide burr bit. Again, great care must be taken with a light touch so that the bit doesn't "run off" causing irreparable gouges in the bines.

After substantially enough material is removed use a small (1/4 inch) drum sander to smooth over the groove marks made by the burr. Proceed to the five sanding grits of Vitex ropes, sanding all surfaces to completion. Turn a base of pink ivory and apply wipe-on polyurethane.

Yellow Heart

The second very thin twist is the most difficult to do. Yellow heart was chosen as an interesting contrast (ultimately a very poor choice because of its fracturing qualities and subsequent weaknesses as a very thin open twist). Since the bore hole is 11/16 inches the yellow heart dowel requires the same diameter with a length of 7-1/2 inches (the extra 1/2 inch is for gluing into the base). Before the dowel is turned a 3/16 inch bore hole needs to be drilled as was done for the thin open twist variant. The stock is then turned between centers to the 11/16 inch diameter.

Mark out a right-handed double twist, then proceed with the 3/16 inch round rasp until close to breakthrough. Make sure to insert a 3/16 inch dowel into the lumen for internal support. Using the small microplane gingerly rasp out the coves while supporting the stock with the free hand.

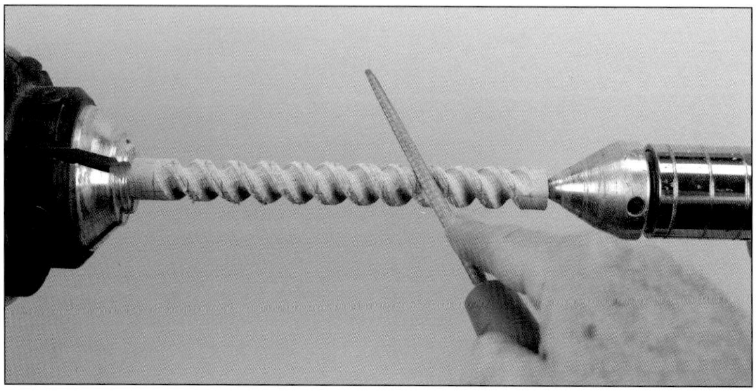

Carefully file over the sharp bine edges.

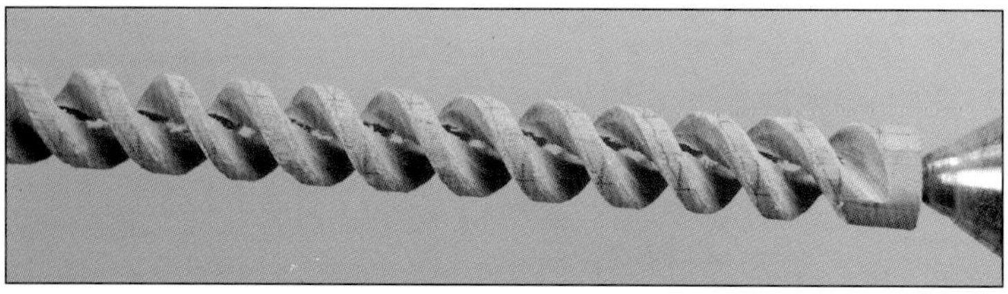

Next, rasp to the lumen. Remove the interior dowel to view the open twist.

Drill with the 11/16 inch aircraft drill bit several pieces of 1-1/4 inch hardwood dowel to be used as external supports then slip both external and internal supports on before sanding is started.

Carefully sand all surfaces with Vitex sanding ropes, moving interior and exterior supports back and forth as needed. Be sure to support the piece with the free hand as well.

The interior dowel support will need to be removed to sand at the ends. [Note: Sanding is most difficult and a very light touch is needed. In spite of care taken, I broke seven very thin twists of yellow heart after 4 to 5 hours of work, causing in most instances, an outburst of righteous indignation and rancorous expletives that would make a sailor blush.] The finish of very thin open twists is polyurethane.

It is most difficult to use wipe-on polyurethane with such a fragile piece. In this one instance the spray-on poly (using a painter's respirator mask) is utilized. The final step is turning a blackwood dowel 3/16 inches diameter and 7-1/2 inches long.

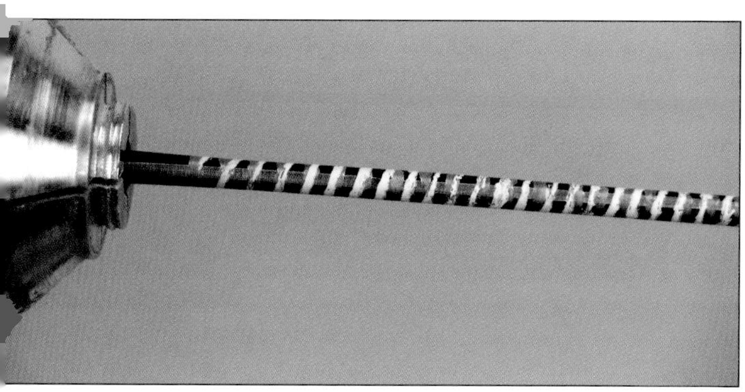

Marking the layout for the left-handed single twist is most difficult.

Some may wish to free hand the twist. External supports, as were used for the double, are needed when carefully rasping with the 3/16 and 1/8 inch round rasps.

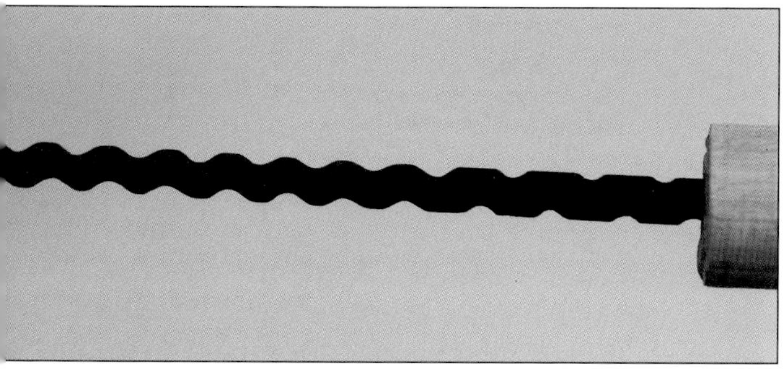

As the project proceeds a nice, subtle single twist is produced. After sanding to completion, use the wipe-on polyurethane to finish the blackwood twist.

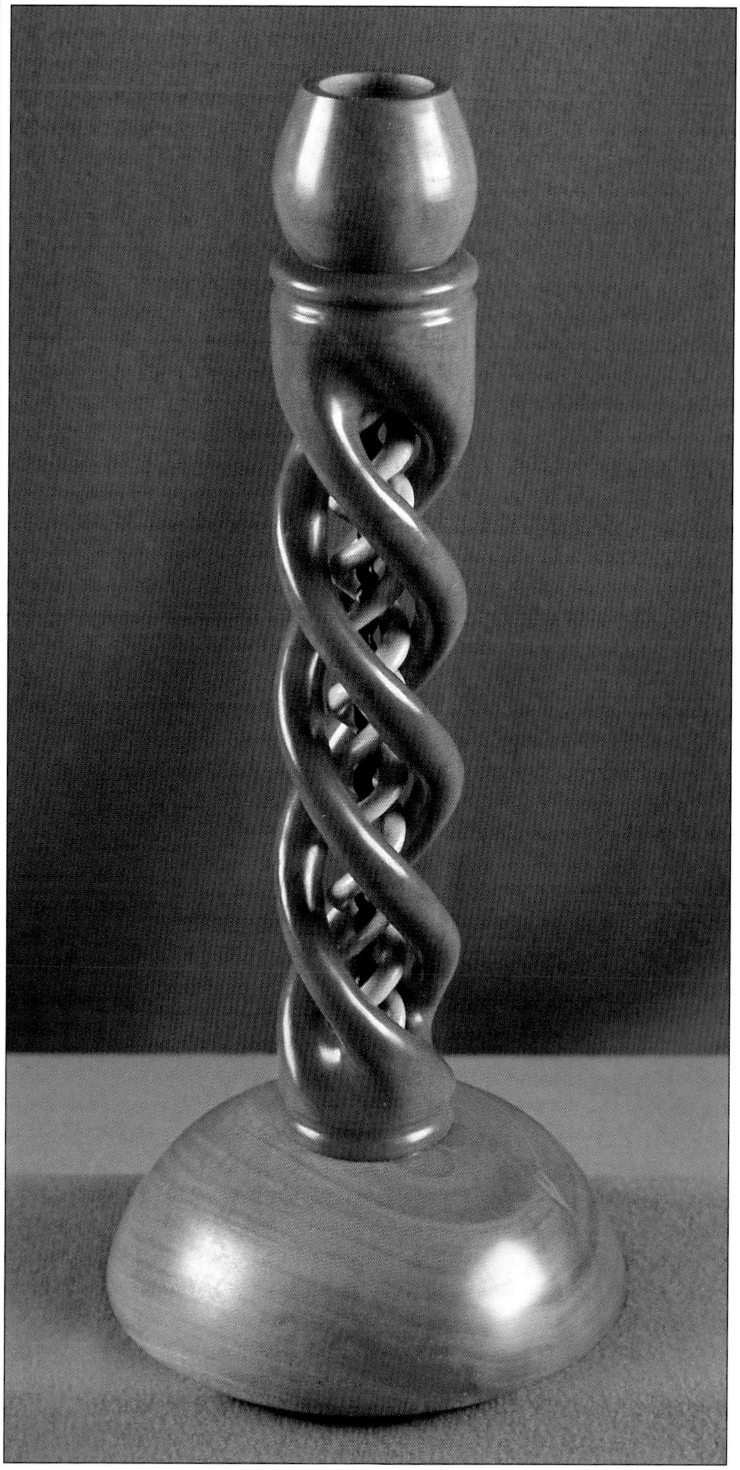

Carefully assemble the single blackwood left-handed twist into the open double barley right-handed twist of yellow heart. Glue these two into the left-handed triple open twist of pink ivory with the 11/16 inch dowel extruding 1/2 inch beyond the bottom to be glued into the turned base. A most impressive piece of usable art is created.

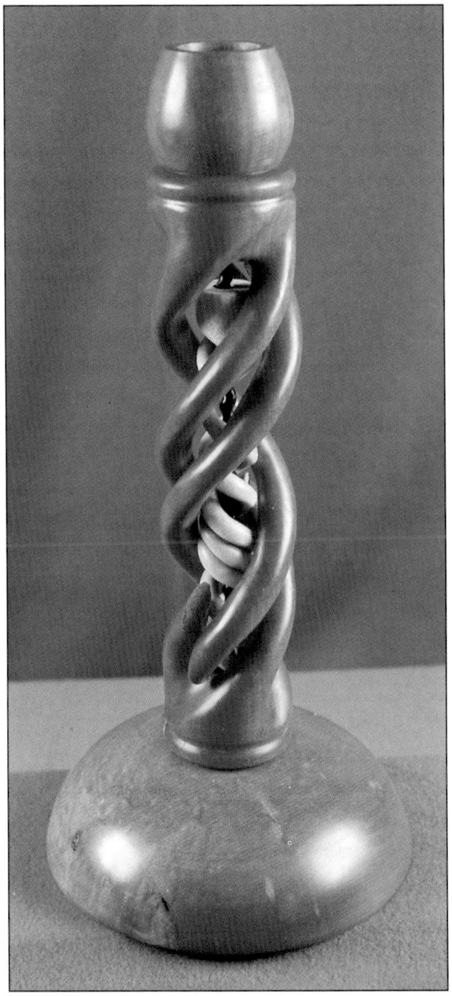

Note in the photo what happens to thirty hours of hard work when one forces the tight fitting glue-up job. The ultimate results are fractured bines and the deep emotion that one is truly on the "off ramp" in the expressway of life. Instances like this necessitate long walks in the garden taking time to smell the roses.

A close-up shows the detail of this extraordinary piece.

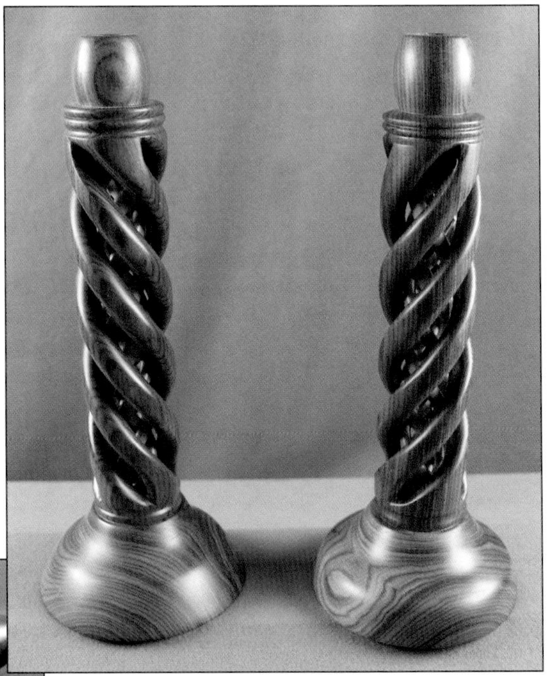

A more prodigious effort is undertaken with the pair of quadruple kingwood open twists with triple pear wood open twists with double holly open twists and single blackwood twists alternating right and left hand with each twist.

A close-up gives more detail of the complexity. That project necessitated the consumption of 90 hours (only three broken open twists during production).

Extremely Thin Twists

It might seem like we're jumping out of the frying pan into the fire as we proceed to extremely thin twists, but, trust me, the worst has passed. We are now in the eye of the hurricane. Extremely thin twists (usually 1/8 inch diameter or less) are usually turned as twisted finials on the tops of decorative boxes made from different exotics (most domestics don't have the inherent strength to accomplish extremely thin twists). The English boxwood stock, partially spalted with elements of burl, is turned between centers, the ends trued-up, a spigot turned on one end to fit the 2 inch O'Donnell jaws, then mounted in the jaws and again, trued-up. A spigot is turned at the distal end to fit the O'Donnell jaws then the basic shape of the box is calculated, turned and the top portion parted off. The top is mounted in the O'Donnell jaws so that the interior of the lid may be hollowed out and a spigot turned to fit into the base. After this is accomplished the finial may be turned. Do not finish the top of the finial before sanding all turned surfaces with various grits of sandpaper. Do not use steel wool as it has the propensity to catch and grab at the ends of the turning piece breaking the stem—the voice of experience speaks here.

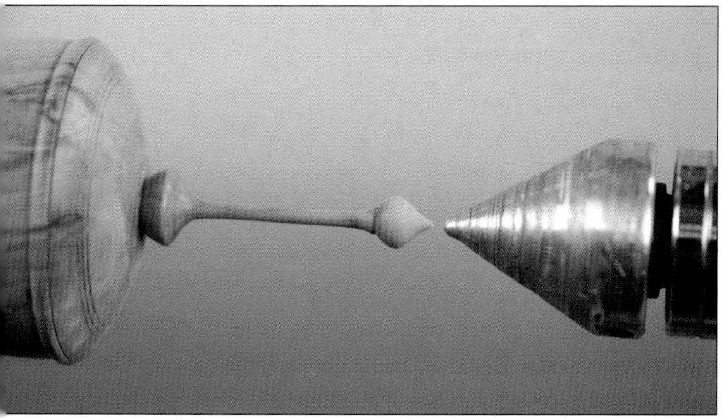

After the piece is sanded, finish turning the Russian onion at the top while supporting the piece with fingers of the free hand.

Next remove the live center end and the point from the cup. If measurement of the Russian onion finial was correctly accomplished, it should just fit into the cup. While carefully rasping and rotating the piece by hand fashion a double barley twist by eye (the piece is much too thin to draw in a layout).

Sand all surfaces with Vitex ropes torn and twisted to form 1/16 inch ropes. Be extremely meticulous in sanding so that the twist doesn't fracture—it will not be repairable if breakage ensues. Be careful when removing the piece from the lathe.

Apply the finish of choice and voila: bodacious boxes are created. From left to right: a tulipwood box with single right-handed twist, a boxwood box with right-handed double barley ribbon twist, and red lace box with right-handed double barley twist.

CHAPTER 4

SCALLOP-EDGED VASES, BOWLS, PLATES, AND PLATTERS

Scallop-Edged Vases

Unlike the last chapters' projects, making a scallop-edged vase can be accomplished on a weekend afternoon while scrutinizing one's favorite team pummel their key rival on TV. The vase's simplicity, gracefulness and recherché appearance adds to the limpid endeavor.

Proper timber selection is once again important and dense woods such as grapefruit (or other citrus woods), mesquite, cocobolo, or domestic hardwoods may be utilized. Softer woods such as masur birch, koa, or redwood burl can be employed if one takes utmost care in forming the twist and hollowing the vase.

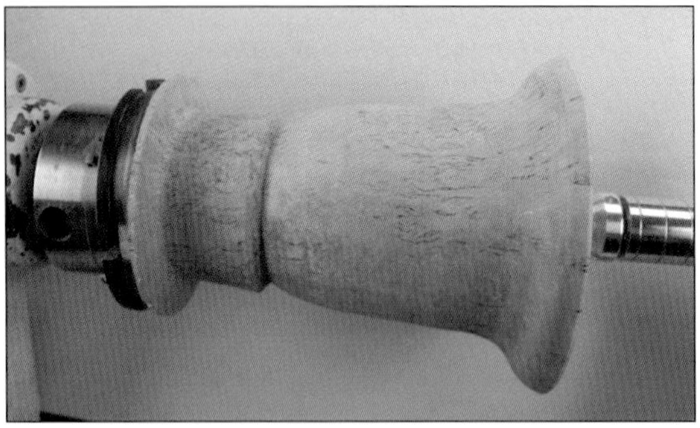

An inchoate log (10" in diameter by 12" long) of masur birch is turned to a cylinder between centers, the ends squared, a spigot cut to fit the Oneway #4 or comparable jaws—it is very important to have a firm grip as the vase will be projecting 16 inches out from the headstock when being hollowed—and a basic vase shape formed with the tailstock brought up for support.

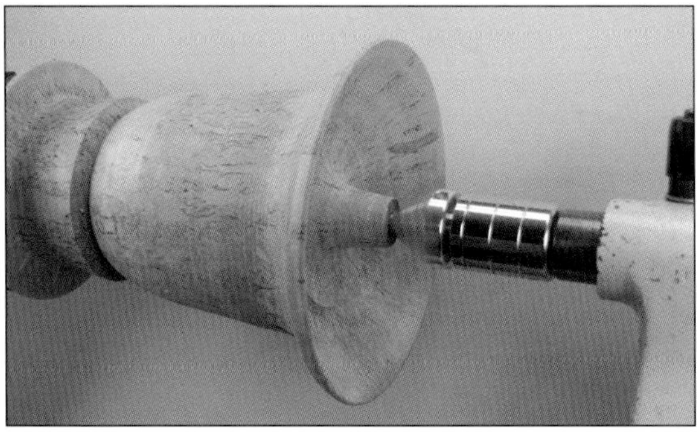

The next step is to turn a concavity simulating the outside contour to a depth of 1-1/2 inches leaving a center cone for support. [Remember you are turning end grain and consequently should start from the center and move to the periphery with your cuts.] Sometimes the tailstock needs to be backed off to adequately reach the center.

A bowl steady may be utilized for support to reduce harmonic vibrations while turning.

After the proper contours (inside and outside) of the lip are formed (thickness of 1/4 to 5/16 inches) it is time to drill holes for the spiral. Turn off or unplug the lathe and utilize the indexing system to obtain equal spacing for drilled holes. [Oneway manufactures a wonderful drill steady able to be adjusted to exact drill depths and angles utilizing the standard tool rest. If you don't have a drill-steady, carefully support the drill on the tool rest for drilling, being careful not to foul the drill bit on the tool rest.]

Using the 48 point indexing system, drill an angled 3/16 inch hole one inch from the lip's edge at each index stop. This will give 48 angled openings. [The reason for angled drilled holes is to set the proper slope for sanding the cut coves with Vitex ropes.] Go back and make a pencil line along the vase's edge at each index stop.

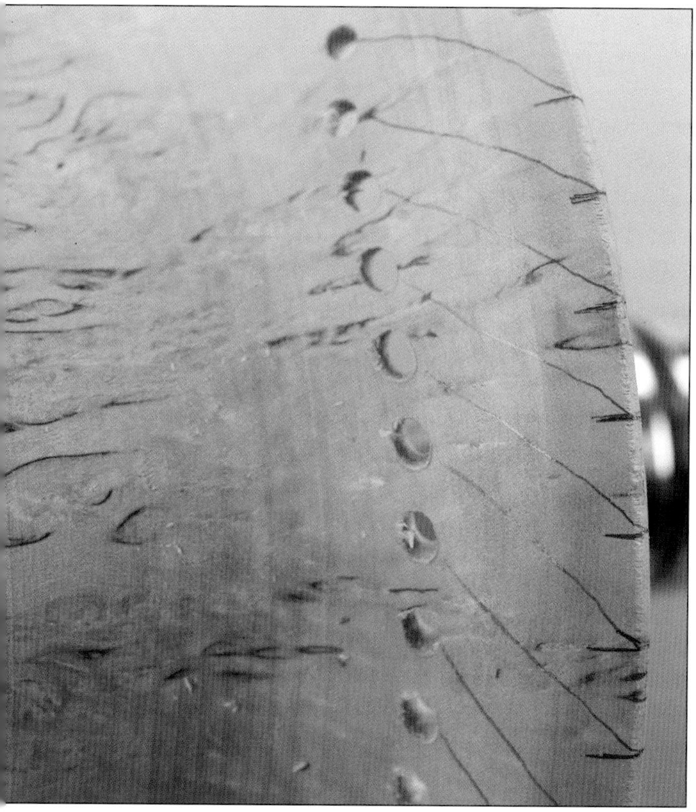

Draw a pencil line from a drilled hole to a second hole's pencil line below the first hole skipping the adjacent hole's pencil line. This will denote the outside spiral cut lines.

Next draw a pencil line on the inside lip from one hole's peripheral line backward to the second adjacent hole. This will give an appearance of finger-like scalloped edges when completed.

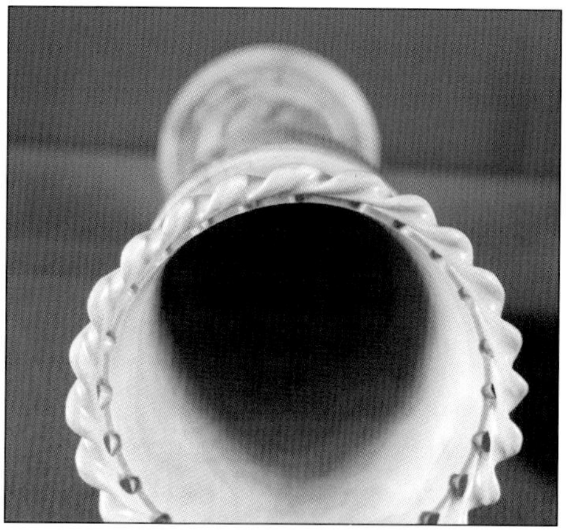

If you draw the lines forward instead of backward the appearance would be of a twisted spiral such as those presented in the grapefruit vase.

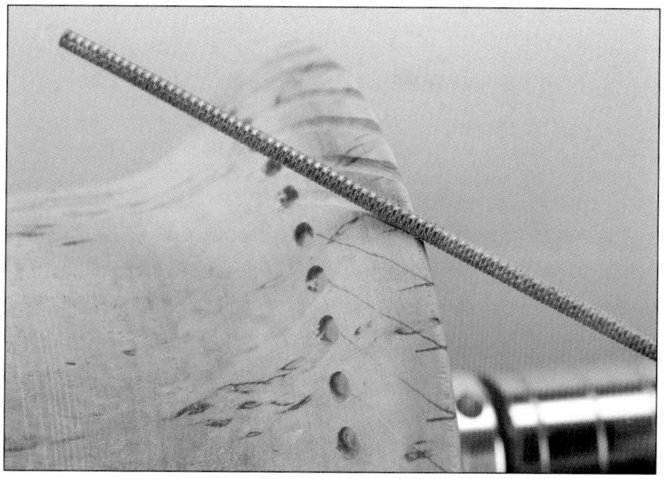

Using the 3/16 inch round rasp cut an angled groove along the drawn outside pencil lines to the drilled hole at each marked pencil line. Be careful not to foul the rasp on the vase beyond the drilled holes.

After the outside grooves are completed rasp the inside in the same manner being careful to make a smooth transition from the lip's edge to the interior grooves.

Sand all cut surfaces using the Vitex sanding ropes from 80 to 400 grit utilizing the angled drill holes to brace the ropes.

After the fingers are sanded smooth use the bowl steady for a brace and drill a one inch diameter hole to the bottom of the vase (7 inches deep) utilizing the compressed-air aircraft drill bit. This process will make it easier to hollow out the vase.

The Jamieson hollowing system shown here, or comparable hollowing systems by Stuart, Sorby, or others, may be utilized to complete the inside of the vase. Remember—hollowing is much easier if you stand on the other side of the lathe and hollow left-handedly.

Complete the inside by sanding with various grit sandpapers. With a large enough opening, power sanding with smaller pads and disks is possible. Fashion the outside vase form with several beads or accents and a spheroid base above the foot while utilizing the Oneway neoprene covered cone live center tailstock piece to protect the vase's interior timber from marks.

With the lathe turned off mark 24 indexed horizontal start lines on the sphere.

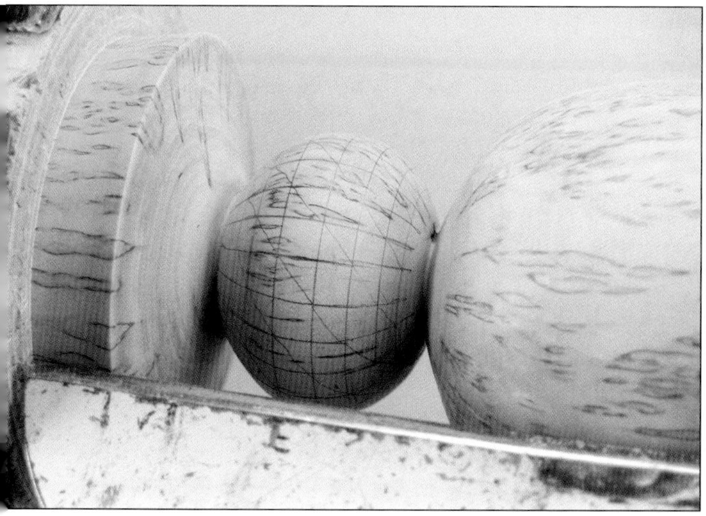

Mark several pitch lines on the sphere with spacing narrower at the poles—this allows a pleasing smooth continuous transition from pole to pole when the cut lines are drawn. Note—when placing spirals on spheres they look best if the spiral extends no more than 1/3 of the circumference.
The cut lines are drawn in every other trapezoid (a rectangle on a sphere's surface becomes a trapezoid unless it is at the equator) at the tailstock towards the headstock giving 12 right-handed twists—it may be noted that in the first 3 chapters we have been working on a two dimensional plane rolled into a cylinder. Here we are definitely working in three dimensional topography.

After all cut lines are drawn protect the vase's bottom with masking tape and be careful not to foul the foot when rasping the grooves with the 1/8 inch rasp. Cut from both right and left of the cut lines. Sand all rough surfaces to completion then carefully part off the foot.

Sand the bottom of the foot and apply a finish of wipe-on polyurethane.

Vase Variants

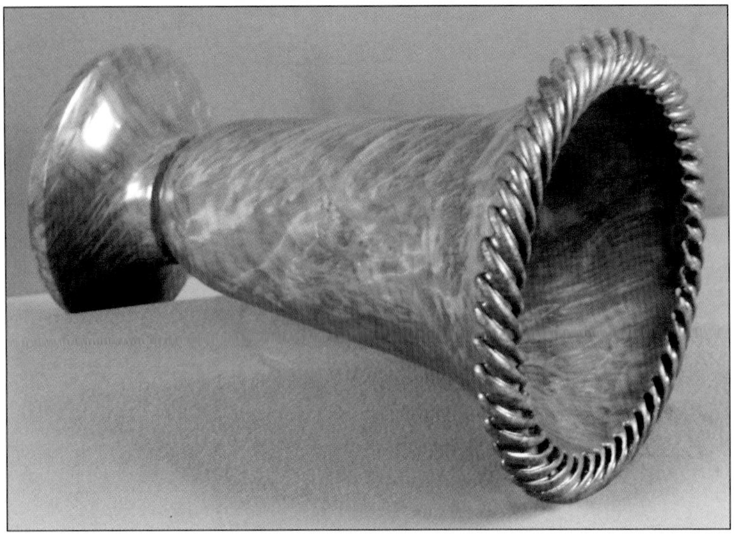

If the vase's lip is rolled over instead of flared out, a most interesting effect can be created in timber such as redwood burl. However, on this piece, only the lip's surface has a twist. The underside is smooth—it is nearly impossible to carve a twist in extremely narrow hidden concavities.

Other types of twists, described previously, are displayed with the scalloped fingered and rolled-over twists.

Scallop-Edged Bowls

Rather interesting applications of twists may be applied to either closed- or opened-form bowls. A good stable timber, such as madrone burl, renders lovely finished bowls. Remember—madrone burl is best turned if it is pressure cooked at 17 psi, 212 degrees for 2 hours, soaked in boiling water for 1 hour, green turned, and let dry for about 6 months otherwise it cracks.

An 11 inch closed-form bowl (lip rolled in instead of out as was demonstrated by the redwood burl vase) is turned to 1/4 inch thickness, sanded to completion and mounted by its foot in the Oneway #3 or comparable jaws.

Utilizing a 48 point indexer, 3/16 inch angled holes are drilled at each index stop one inch from the bowl's lip. Orange start lines are drawn horizontally at each drill hole to the rolled interior lip's edge. Orange pitch lines are drawn and then green cut lines from bottom to top in every trapezoid are drawn. Essentially 2 drilled holes are skipped to give a pleasing spiral.

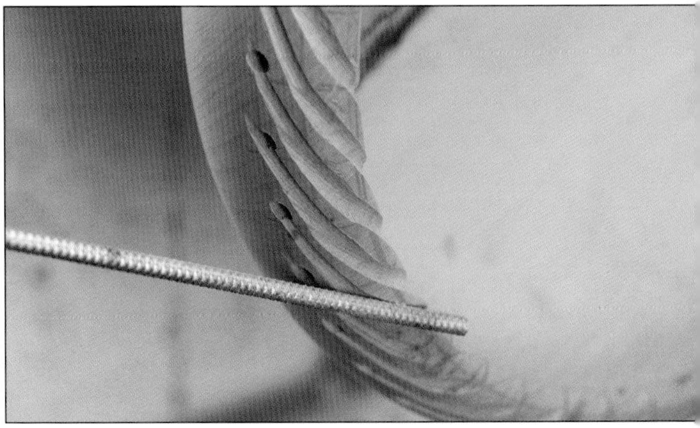

Next, utilizing the 3/16 inch rasp, cut grooves along the 48 cut lines. After the rasped grooves are completed, sand all surfaces with Vitex ropes employing the drilled holes.

Note: The under surface of the lip is not sanded but the lip's top grooves are, as noted in the photo.

After the sanding is complete, apply wipe-on polyurethane for a finished product.

Scallop-Edged Bowl Variant

An impressive large bowl of 22 inch diameter madrone burl stock may present an intriguing demeanor when its smoothed-out, angled, flattened lip is scalloped by twists. The key technique is to turn the large bowl to a 1/4 inch wall thickness, but undercut the flat 1-1/4 inch inward tapered lip so that interesting shadows may be cast as light shines on the bowl. It also has an appearance of being heavy until someone happens to pick it up and is amazed by its buoyancy and delicacy.

Since the bowl is so large, 96 points need to be drawn with the indexer. The easiest approach is to draw 48 horizontal orange pencil start lines utilizing the tool rest at dead center height, interpolate the equi-distant point between a pair of orange start lines, loosen the 4 jaws, rotate the bowl to the marked equi-distant point, then tighten the chuck jaws. The next 48 start lines may be drawn utilizing the index stops. If one needs even more points or one has only 12 or 24 index stops, interpolation with 3 or 6 points could be employed by marking and rotating the stock in the chuck's jaws.

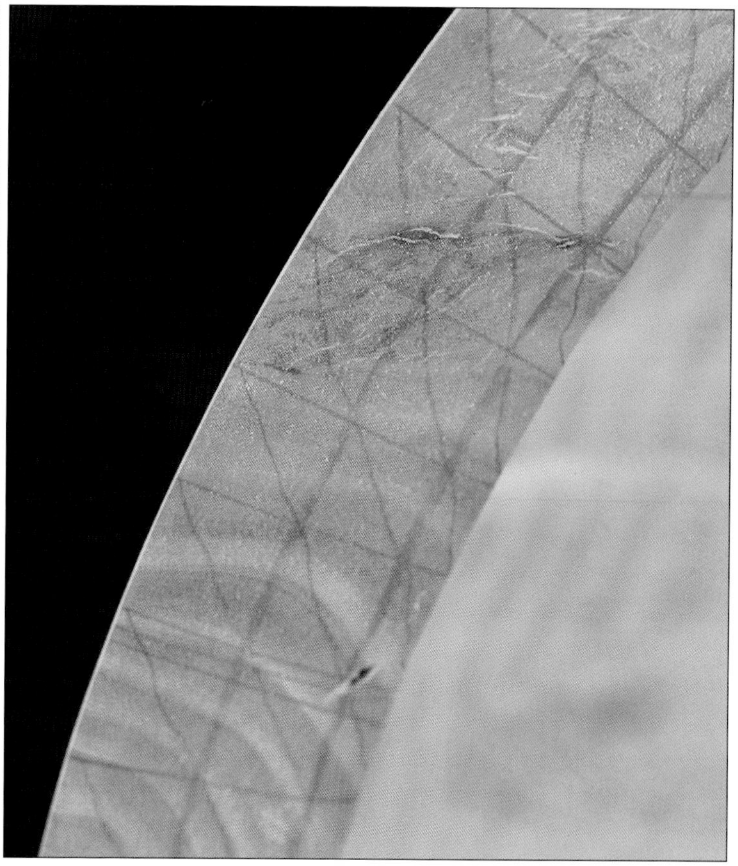

After the start lines are drawn, draw several pitch lines with an orange pencil making the spaces narrower towards the center of the bowl. Draw a blue line from bottom right to top left corners of each trapezoid continuing into the above angled trapezoid (a true rectangle has 2 pair of equal sides—our trapezoid has only one pair because it is a rectangle living on a curve).

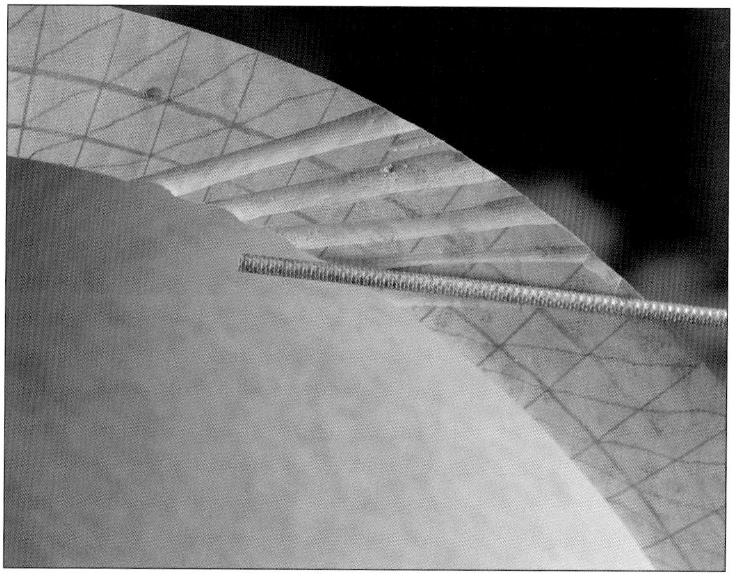

Next rasp the blue cut lines with a 3/16 inch rasp.

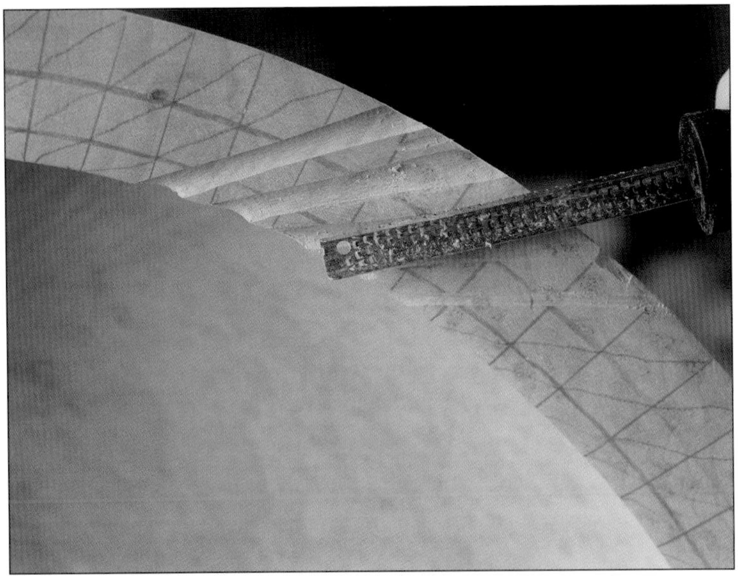

Use the small microplane to cut a deeper wider cove on the outside edge tapered towards the center of the bowl. Cut from outside inward.

After all 96 coves are formed use Vitex ropes to sand all surfaces.

After applying the wipe-on polyurethane a beautiful large artistic bowl is presented.

Scallop-Edged Plates

Intellectual compulsivity mandates a brief digression for a semi-erudite pontification of variances between plates and platters. The English maintain plates have proportionally greater height to diameter than platters but a society that took over 100 years to complete its dictionary should have its opinions brought into question. Besides, who made the English the plate or platter police? Webster states a platter is a large plate used usually for serving. A plate is a flat object of wood or metal used to hold food for an individual. A dish is a plate made of china or glass.

Step one is to turn a disk true so that a waste block may be glued to the backside then mounted to an off-centered chuck. The one demonstrated is the Axminster off-centered chuck. There are 9 screw holes on one side of the ring and one on the opposite side. By loosening them and moving the screw to the left or right of the median screw hole an off-centered mount may be obtained. There are 3 screw holes in the center of the mounting disk at 0, 120, and 240 degrees. I always keep them numbered #1, #2, and #3. By marking the waste block as well rotation of these positions may be easily had. The off-centered chuck is mounted on the 2-1/2 inch dovetail Axminster or comparable jaws.

With that catharsis we will discuss the production of a scalloped edged plate with off-centered inlays.

With the lathe turning at 200-300 rpms use a 2-1/4 inch Forstner drill bit to drill a 7/8 inch deep hole. After turning a 2-1/4 inch diameter piece of yellow heart true glue it into the drilled hole. When the glue dries drill a 1-3/4 inch diameter Forstner bit hole and glue in the same sized piece of blackwood. Loosen the Axminster chuck, take off the plate, loosen the 3 center screws in the waste block and rotate to the screw holes 120 degrees to the right.

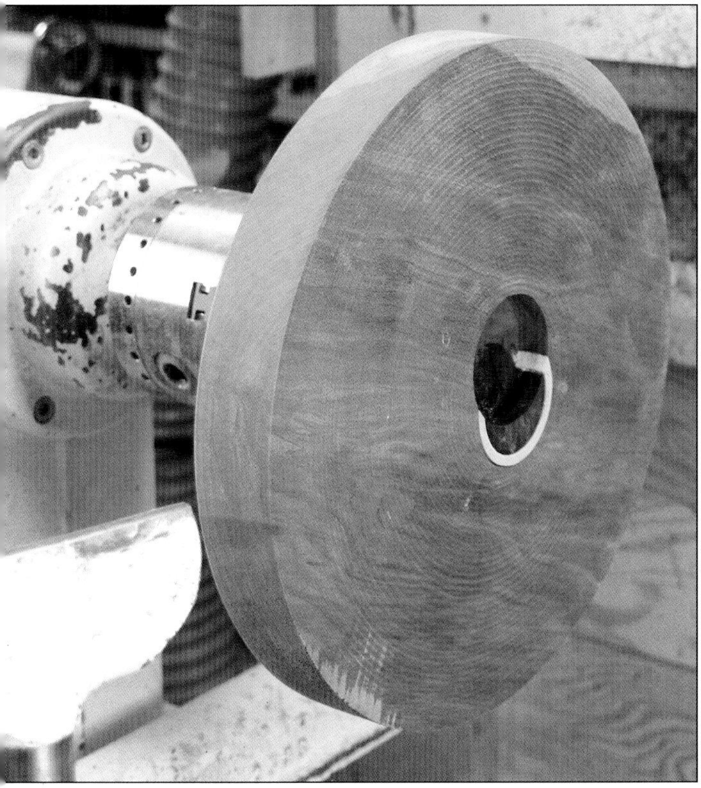

Remount the stock and drill with the 2-1/4 inch Forstner bit another hole. Glue in the same sized blackwood disk.

After the glue is dry drill a 1-3/4 inch diameter hole and glue in the same sized holly disk. Turn the glued pieces flat then remove the stock, rotate the off-centered disk right to the next 120 degree rotation and remount the plate. Drill a third hole 2-1/4 inches and glue in a holly disk. After the glue dries drill a 1-3/4 inch hole and glue in another contrasting disk. When the glue is dry remove the stock and center the off-center screw to the median screw hole.

Remount the stock and drill a 1-1/4 inch hole, glue in a contrasting disk then turn the face true.

Next turn a rebate to fit the #4 One-way dovetail or comparable jaws.

Mount the disk in the 4-jaws and turn the backside of the plate to completion with a rebate to mount in 2-1/2 inch dovetail jaws. Remount the plate and turn the face side to completion. Remember to taper the plate's lip inward slightly so that the lip doesn't look flat or tapered outward—an optical "conclusion" from the topography.
After sanding apply wipe-on polyurethane. Note—I like to apply the polyurethane finish to darker woods so that a silver Sharpie can be used for marking the layout and won't bleed into the wood.

After mounting the finished plate use the 48 point indexer to drill 3/16 inch holes along the backside of the plate.

Mark start points at each index stop on the lip's edge.

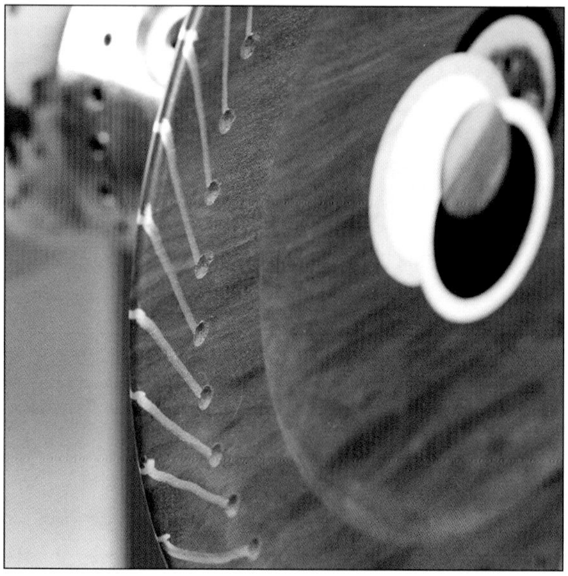

Draw cut lines from the start point mark to the second adjacent hole going top toward bottom on the radius.

Do the same for the backside only go from bottom to top so that a spiral may be produced.

Use a 1/8 inch rasp to cut along the front cut lines.

Use the same rasp to cut along the backside cut lines.

This produces an interesting spiral.

Sand all groove surfaces front and back.

The front of the plate is quite handsome.

The back of the plate presents a pleasing appearance as well.

Plate Variants

Another interesting appearance can be had if no drill holes are utilized in the plate. A red heart plate is turned to completion, sanded and finished with wipe-on polyurethane and mounted in 2-1/2 inch dovetail jaws.

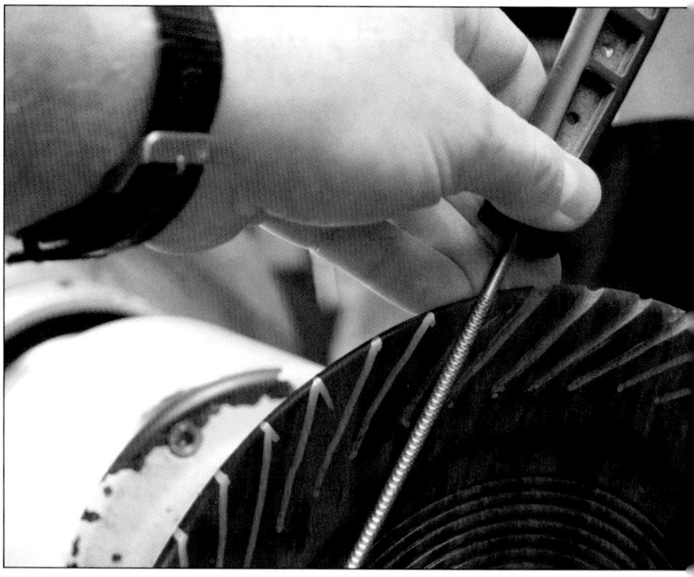

Use the 1/8 inch rasp to cut grooves along the silver cut lines from the periphery in, while bracing the cutting hand on the plate.

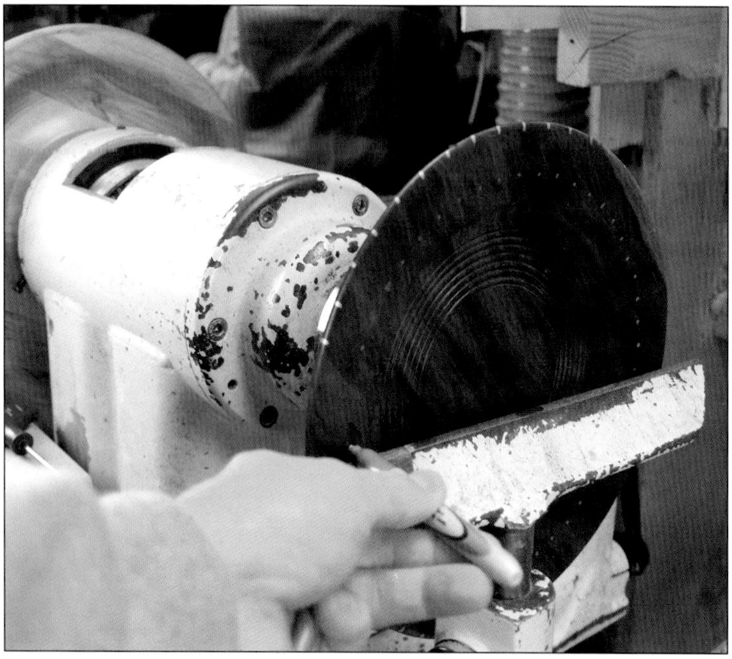

Using the 48 point indexer mark silver spots on the plate's edge and one inch from the edge.

Upon completion of the grooves, sand with Klingspor rolls from 80 to 400 grit.

Cut lines are then drawn from the outside mark to the second, lower inside mark.

Apply a wipe-on finish to the sanded grooves for a nice finished scallop-edged plate variant.

The backside is as pleasing as the front.

Scallop-Edged Stained Platters

Platters are similar to plates only larger in diameter—remember the definitions. Platters that are about 16-17 inches in diameter make the most functional pieces and are easier to hang on the wall. If the platter (or plate for that matter) is turned out of a solid piece it must be turned with quarter-sawn wood or it will warp due to the stresses in the wood. As a consequence I like to utilize pieces of quarter-sawn curly or quilted maple sandwiched together with black-dyed, 1/16 inch thick maple veneer between. It adds accents as well as interesting patterns and, coupled with water-based aniline dye gel stains, a most pleasing artistic flair for usable platters and/or wall hangings. It is what I refer to as practical art.

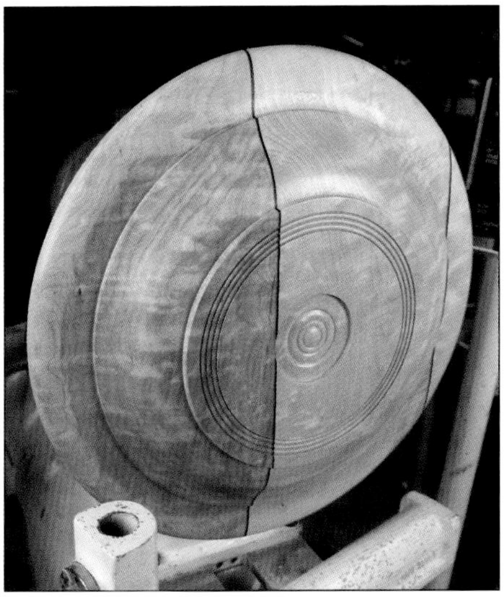

Since we will be using a water-based gel stain, the portion of the platter that will not be stained must be finished with our polyurethane so any stain that smears over it can easily be wiped off. The underside and frontside lips are to be stained and twisted.

The first step is drilling 48 holes at the interior lip's border as well as marking a pencil line at the periphery. Re-chuck the platter using the rebate turned in its bottom and turn the front side of the lip.

Interpolate an equi-distant point between 2 of the drilled holes, loosen the chuck's jaws, and rotate to the mark. Drill another 48 holes using the drill master and indexer. Also mark the periphery as before.

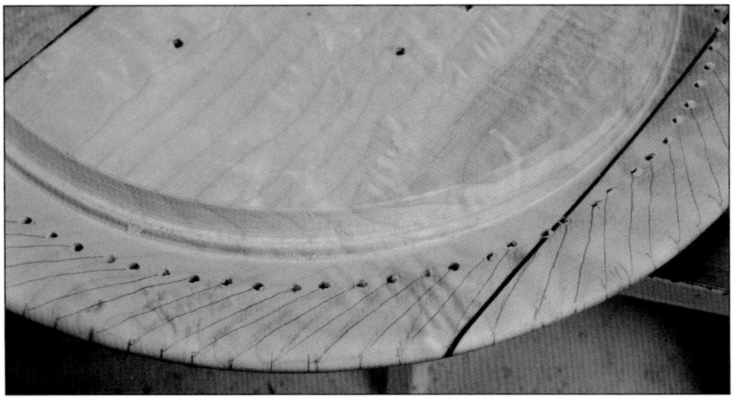

After the 96 holes are drilled remove the platter and draw a pencil cut line from the peripheral line to the third hole to the right.

Draw all 96 cut lines. Turn the platter over and do the same for the backside of the lip. Use the 3/16 inch rasp to cut coves being careful to have a smooth transition at the lip's edge. Sand all surfaces with Vitex ropes to completion.

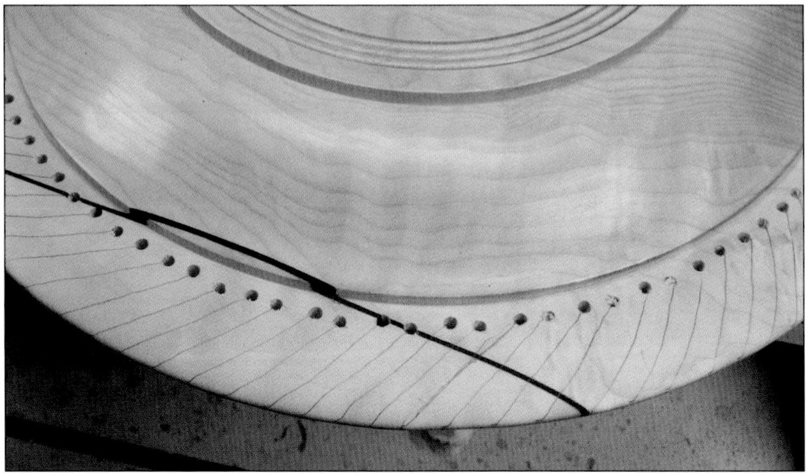

The next step entails using a thin paint brush to apply blue gel stain to the holes and, with a larger brush, to the twists (front and back). Don't worry about getting stains towards the interior front of the platter as that wood will be turned off later.

After all surfaces are colored, wipe off the excess gel with a clean cloth removing any lumps. Double check to make sure every area to be stained is stained evenly. The gel stain dries in approximately one minute and any finish can be applied in about 1 hour.

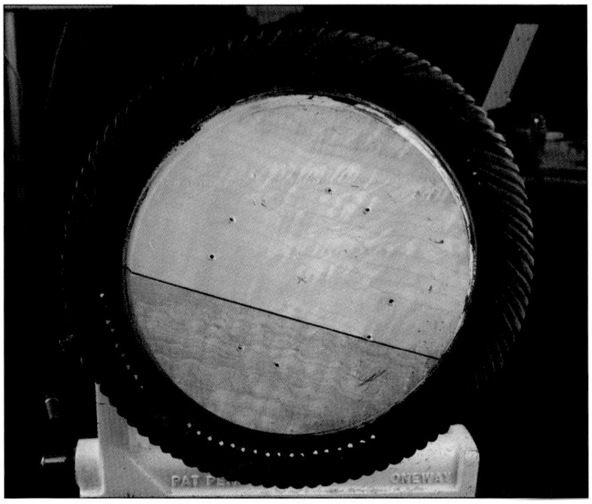

Next, paint on green with a broad brush so that the holes and coves will remain blue.

Wipe off the excess so that an interesting turquoise-blue pattern remains.

Turn the platter to completion, power sand the center, and apply a finish to yield a practical piece of precious art.

Another type of platter similar to the plate demonstrated earlier may be fashioned whenever the lip is rolled over. The backside must be finished with polyurethane as no stain is to be applied on it.
With the platter mounted, curved tool rest dead centered, and interior depth mark on the tool rest (blue tape) use the 48 point index to mark a pencil line at the edge and in about 1-1/2 inch.

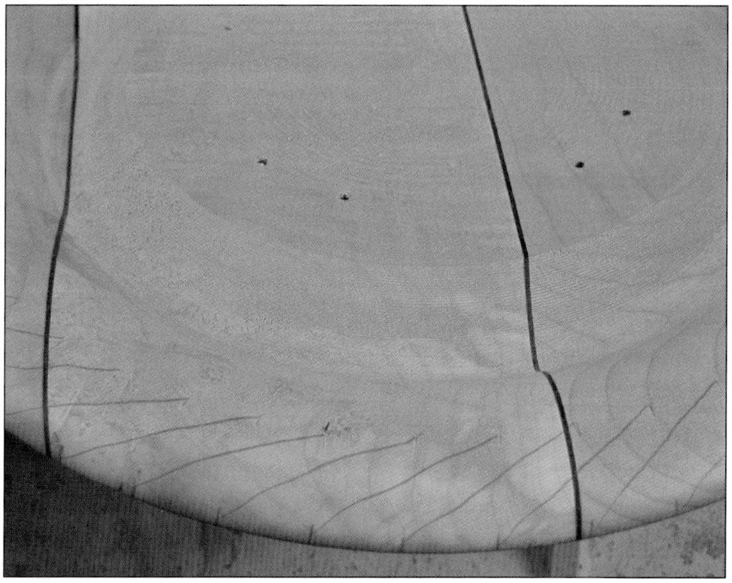

Mark with a red pencil from the plate's edge to the second pencil mark to the right cut lines for all 48 points.

Next use the small microplane to rasp out coves cutting from the edge towards the interior and making slightly deeper broader grooves at the lip's edge.

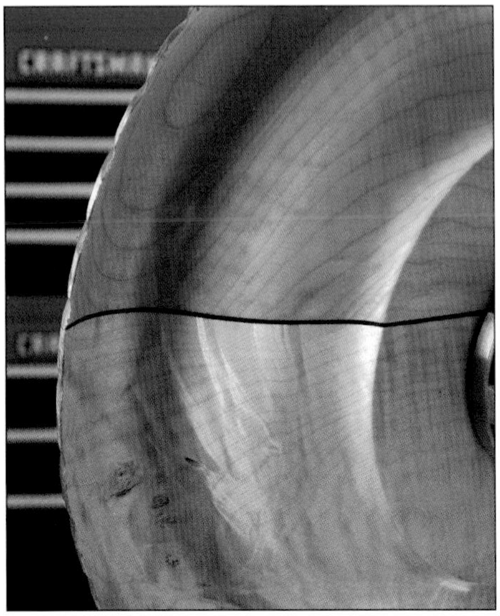

Apply a red gel stain to all surfaces but be sure to wipe any excess off the polyurethaned backside.

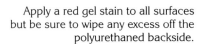

Apply a purple gel stain to the surface with a broad brush so that the coves remain red. Wipe off the excess and complete the interior of the platter.

After power sanding apply the finish for another beautiful bodacious piece.

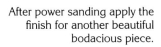

CHAPTER 5

HAND THREAD CHASING

Any book about spiral turnings would not be complete without mentioning hand thread chasing. After all, a thread is merely a single twist with an extremely low grade pitch. A fitted pair of threads is nothing more than one object's bines fitting into its mate's coves giving a firm but easily unwound connection. Threads were extensively used by master turners to screw together assorted pieces before the advent of cyanoacrylate glues. Now there are only a few turners using and teaching hand thread chasing but there is renewed interest in the technique.

Hand thread chasing is a curious technique that may be compared to riding a bicycle or driving a car. One can read extensively about it or observe a person doing it but until the individual actually accomplishes the task it can't be mastered. As a consequence narratives and videos are poor seconds to hands-on experience.

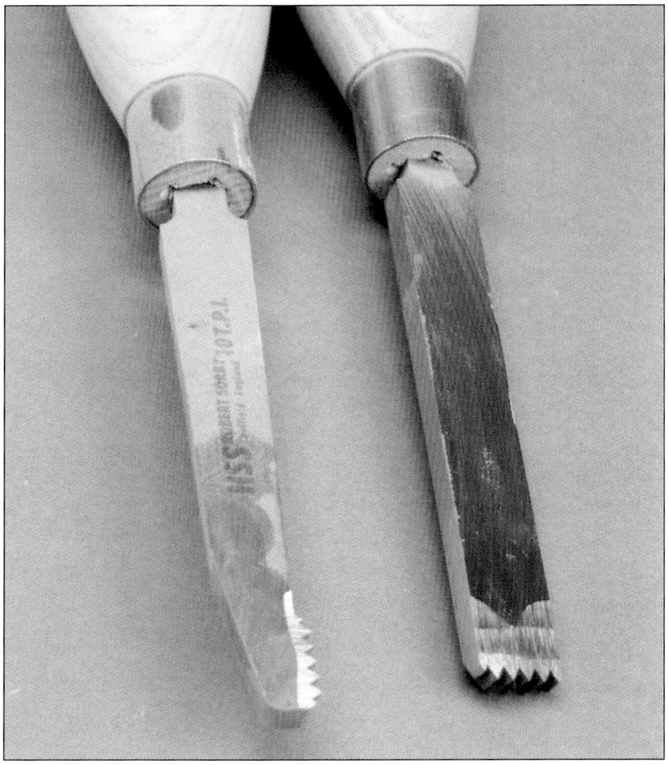

The first task is to select the proper set of thread chasers. They come in pairs—female and male—and vary in the size of threads created per inch. The most popular sizes are 20, 18, and 16 TPI (threads per inch) but sometimes larger threads are desired such as 10 or 12 TPI.

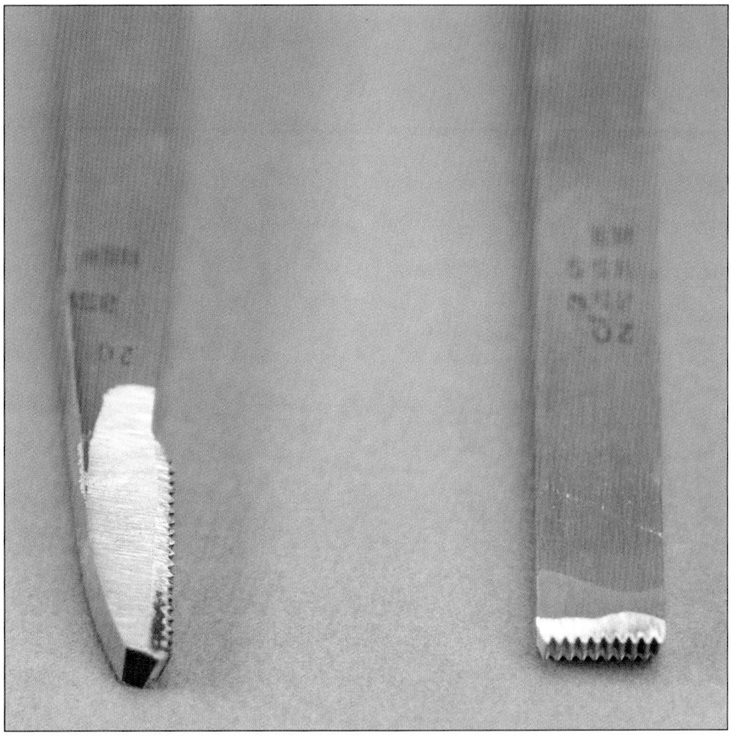

After purchasing the set one must do some grinding in order to have the chasers function properly. The female chaser (we're talking tools here) needs its distal side opposite the teeth ground down to a taper so that it may fit into small holes and still function. Never sharpen the teeth but place a hollow grind on the toothed side top as noted in the photos.
The same hollow grind on top is used for the male chaser as well (above two photos right side). It is also prudent to round over the underside of the first and last teeth to avoid catches when chasing.

The selection of material is most important. One cannot chase soft woods. A dense greasy wood works best but some synthetic substances may prove adequate. Epoxy laced with a trace of aniline dye set in turned rebates may produce lovely threads for those who can't afford expensive and rare exotic timbers. One must remember to use a slightly duller chaser so as to not fracture or break the epoxy threads.

The best timber to chase is boxwood, but blackwood, cocobolo, pink ivory, olivewood, rosewoods, lignum vitae, ironwood or other hard woods will work. Brittle woods will fracture and are less than ideal.

When doing male and female threads, mixing different colored woods may give exciting contrasts to the finished product as well as adding strength and longevity to the piece.

My personal preference whether for a lidded hollow form, reliquary, or pierced-through hollow form, is a disc of either boxwood or blackwood turned with a spigot to fit into a rebate at the vessel's opening.

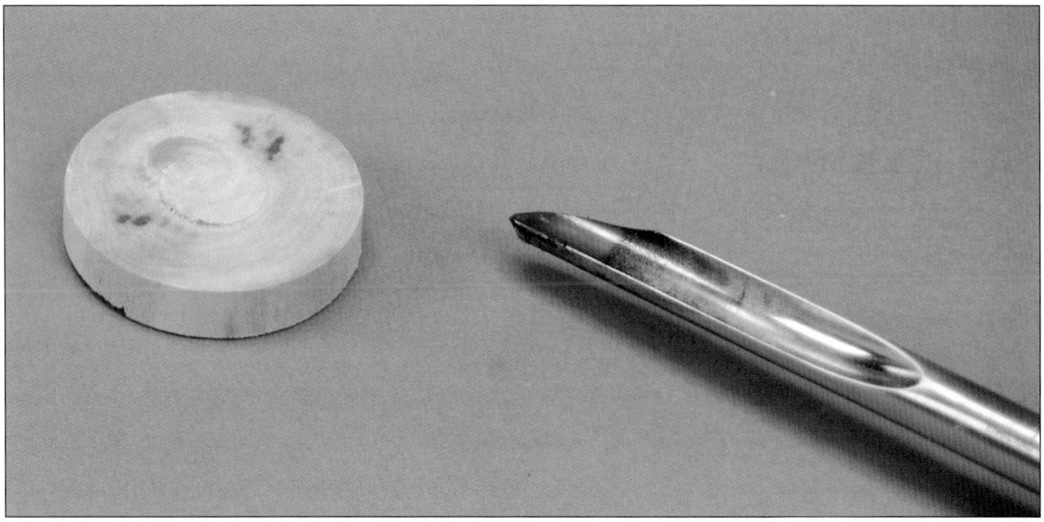

Using a 1/2 inch thick, 2 inch diameter piece of boxwood mounted in the O'Donnell jaws of the Axminster chuck and a 1/2 inch spindle gouge with one side (right) ground down is a good start.

The tool may be used to push like a drill, allowing opening of a hole to thread chase.

Permit me to digress again for a moment to discuss straight and tapered threads. Chasing straight threads is easier but requires an infinite number of turns to tighten or loosen the top piece. If the threaded hole is tapered then oft times a 360 degree turn may suffice to tighten or loosen the top, giving the same surface area and holding power. Of course tapered fits are more difficult to produce. For our demonstration tapered threads are on the menu.

After opening the hole a small square cutter is utilized to cut a tapered opening 1-1/4 inch to 1 inch diameter—**xxx see also photo 218 in chapter 6.**

The opening is approached at a 45 degree angle, kissing the opening edge with the middle of the chaser held parallel to the lathe bed. After several touches a thread will begin to form and the chaser can be lightly advanced.

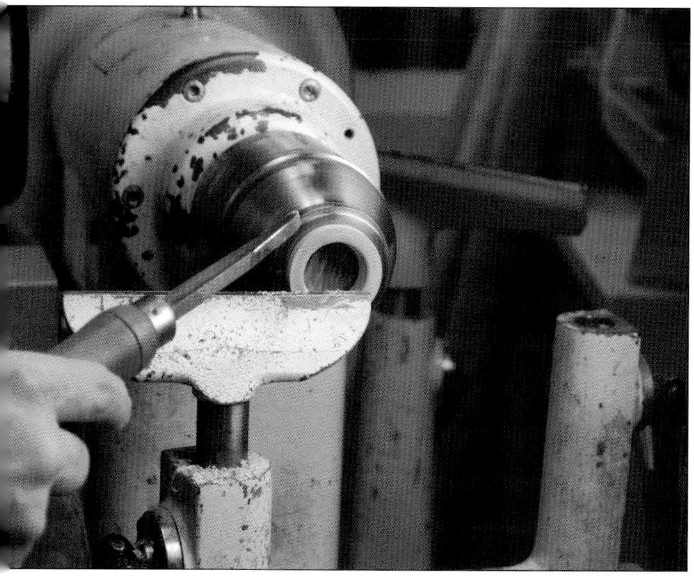

Reduce the rpms of the lathe to about 300. This will allow a reasonable speed to chase the female threads. One should either use a special tool rest or file and sand their singular tool rest to remove nicks, cuts, gobs of glue or other debris which may cause the chaser to run askew.

Continue starting at the opening with the front of the chaser following it through to the bottom of the sleeve.

With several passes an adequate tapered thread is produced.

A toothbrush with hard wax will help polish the threads. A light touch with fine sand paper will knock off the thin tops of the threads allowing easier turning in of the male thread.
The female thread is complete and can be removed from the chuck so that the male portion may be produced.

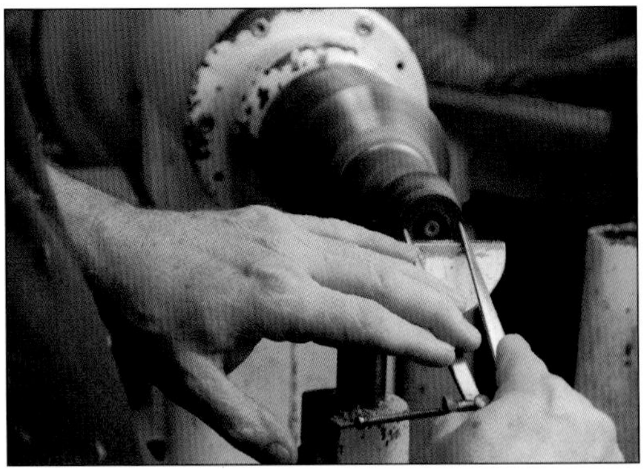

After turning between centers a piece of cocobolo to a cylinder, squaring the ends and turning a 1/8 inch spigot, the stock can be mounted in the O'Donnell jaws. On the squared end mark with calipers a guide circle slightly proud of the top diameter and another of the bottom diameter of the boxwood threaded hole. Next turn a 1/2 inch long spigot the diameter of the large caliper mark. Then taper it to the smaller caliper mark. The turned taper should fit about half way into the threaded sleeve.

Cut a 1/16 inch wide rebate 1/4 inch deep with a narrow parting tool so that a stop is created to keep the male thread chaser from fouling on the bottom of the finial.

Whenever the stop or gap is reached by the leading thread the chaser must be pulled back otherwise it will foul and destroy all chased threads.

Turn the rpms down to 200 for male thread chasing. If one goes slower a wavy or drunken thread may be produced. Using a counterclockwise motion lightly kiss the edge of the taper with the middle of the chaser.

After an adequate fit is created polish the threads with wax as before and lightly touch with fine sand paper to knock off the sharp thread edges.

After several touches a thread will begin to be cut.

The finished thread is ready for completion.

The chaser may be followed up to the rebate and withdrawn before fouling on the finial's base.

Remount the boxwood sleeve and screw in the cocobolo unfinished finial. [The advantage of using a sleeve is; should one make a mistake a new sleeve can be easily made throwing away the old one].

Begin turning off excess timber supporting the piece with the tailstock until nearly finished.

The finished finial may be sanded to complete the project.

A finished straight blackwood sleeve and pink ivory finial are contrasted with the tapered boxwood—cocobolo combination.

CHAPTER 6

PIERCED-THROUGH HOLLOW FORMS AND PIERCED-THROUGH HOLLOW FINIAL THREADED LIDS

As we arrive at this last instructive chapter it will become intuitively obvious to the causal observer that pierced-through projects are not neanic endeavors. It's the same melody but a different instrument. Pierced-through hollow forms require the utmost patience, skill, care, and attention one can possibly muster. Not only are there many opportunities to do bodily harm if concentration is set aside, but all the turner's talents, abilities and actions must be at the forefront of his/her thoughts. Then and only then can a sublime artistic audacious composition be created.

Turning hollow forms is not that difficult. Once again the proper selection of timbers is necessitated to produce a good, stable end product. Trying to turn wet wood to completion won't work. Probably the most reasonable approach is to turn wet timber sometime beforehand in order to let it dry, warp out of round, and get completely through its movement thing—8% shrinkage radial, 4% shrinkage tangentially. If one has the time and space turning several chunks of stock to the proper, pleasing shapes and hollowing them to a wall thickness of 1/2 to 3/4 inches will allow a reasonable compendium of dried timbers to choose from for the projects.

The selected stock is an 8 inch diameter 9 inch tall piece of merismatic maple burl turned 3 years previously to a wall thickness of 3/4 inches. It is mounted by the bottom spigot in large dovetail jaws of the Axminster chuck.

The first step is to square the opening with a small 1/4 inch square rebate tool used in the previous chapter. This will allow the tailstock cone to hold the stock squarely centered. [The opening is made to fit the blackwood sleeve created in chapter 5.]

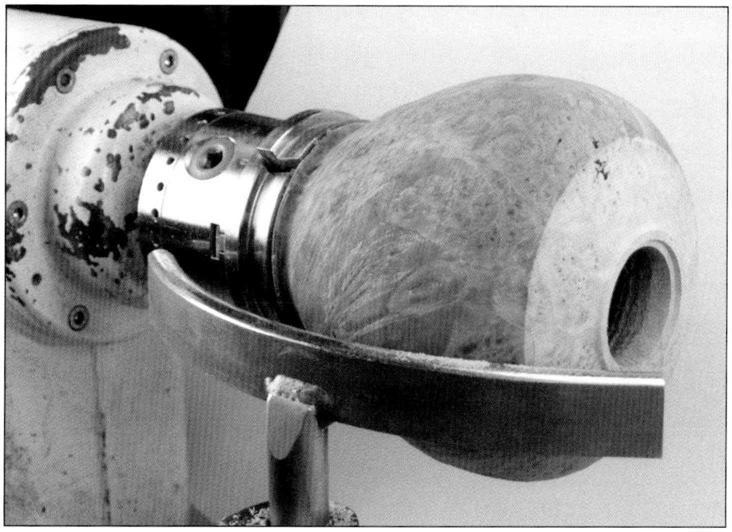

The next step is to round over the opening area removing some of the burl defect with a spindle gouge.

The tailstock can then be brought up so that the hollow form may be turned true.

As with most burls defects and inclusions may be hardened with cyanoacrylate glues. Hand sanding the wet glue allows created sawdust to fill in gaps and become part of the wood.

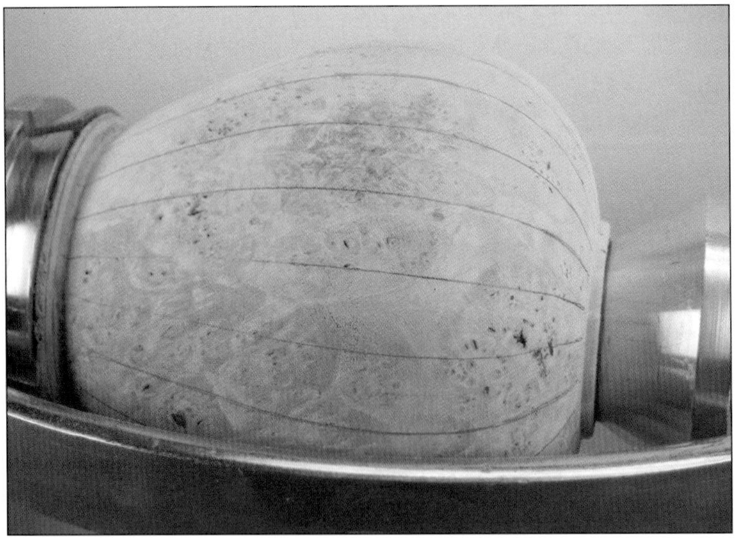

After all defects are fixed, turn off or unplug the lathe and use the indexer to mark out 24 start lines.

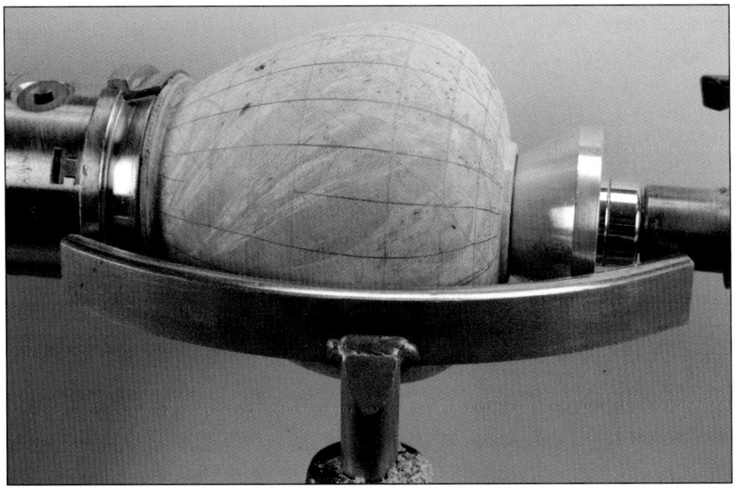

Next are the pitch lines. Remember we are working on the surface of a spheroid so pitch lines near the poles are closer together to give a smooth continuous spiral to the bines. The spiral looks best if the twist covers 25-35% of the spheroid's circumference.

Next mark the cut lines with a red pencil, then with a blue pencil mark the bine lines. There should be 12 blue bine lines and 12 red cut lines.

The next step is very very dangerous!!! With the spindle locked, use both hands to hold the grinder equipped with a small carbide cutting disc to carefully cut through every fourth cut line into the lumen. [It should be noted that the grinder has a propensity to pull forward when cutting. Keep your hands out of the way.] This allows a portal of exit for shavings when truing the inside. Be careful not to hit the chuck and please wear a face shield as well as eye protection. After the 4 portals are completed, finish turning the inside. Hint: if one hollows left-handedly standing on the other side of the lathe, the task is accomplished in a much easier fashion. [If you've ever wondered why the best hollow form producers are left-handed this is the reason.]

Since the bines will be about 1/4 inch thick at the poles and 1/2 inch thick at the equator, the wall thickness of the hollow form must be turned accordingly. [Some turners like the bines to be the same thickness from pole to pole. If you desire this type of bine then the portals need to be cut at a taper towards the poles.]

After the proper thickness is reached (easily discernable by looking at the 4 linear portals) complete the opening of the other 8 cut lines with the adapted grinder while the lathe is off and spindle locked.

Use the grinder to further open the portals.

Next go to the hand-held Foredom tool, equipped with tungsten tapered pencil cutter. With the cutter, round over the tops and bottoms of the bines. It is very difficult to do the undersides and much patience will result in a good end product.

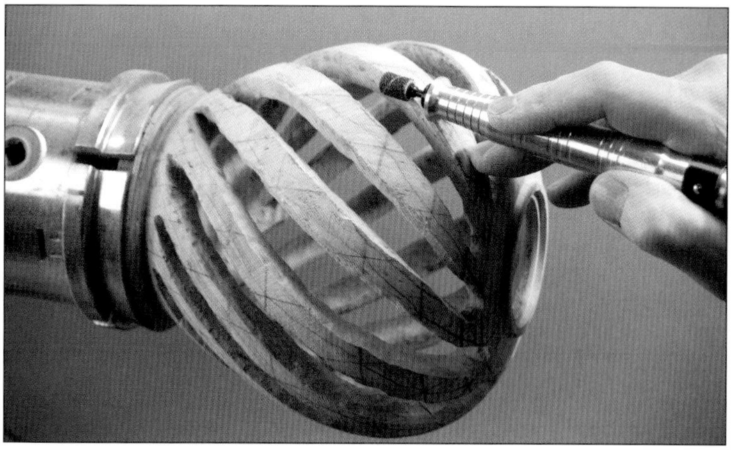

The next step is sanding with a small, coarse drum, changing drums frequently as they become clogged with debris.

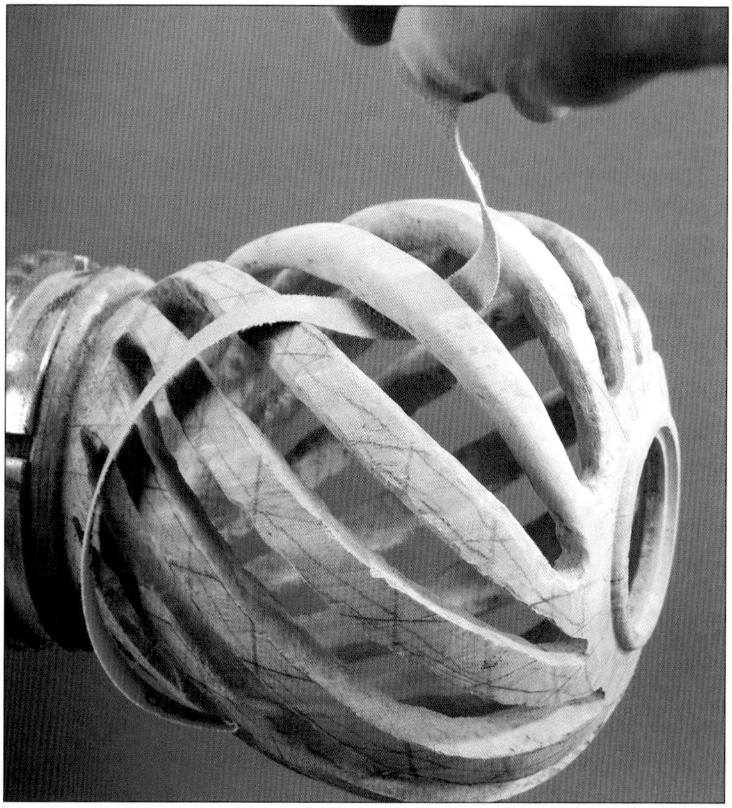

After a bine is drum-sanded, go to the Klingspor sanding tapes to refine the sanding with 80 to 320 grits. Sanding ropes of Vitex will be needed on the bines at either pole. When all bines are sanded use a small disc on an extension power sander to sand the bottom inside of the hollow form.

Reverse chuck the stock in O'Donnell jaws and line up the center point at the tailstock to finish the bottom.

It is best to wrap the bines with masking tape when turning the bottom to protect the bines from centrifugal forces that could fracture them.

After the bottom is fashioned, a small nubbin is left which can be cut off and the excision site sanded smooth. Apply wipe-on polyurethane for a finish and let dry.

Pierced-Through Threaded Hollow Finial

Picking a good, contrasting wood for the finial is necessary to produce an eye-catching product. Since we are using a threaded blackwood sleeve a defect-free cylinder of pink ivory would fit the bill best.

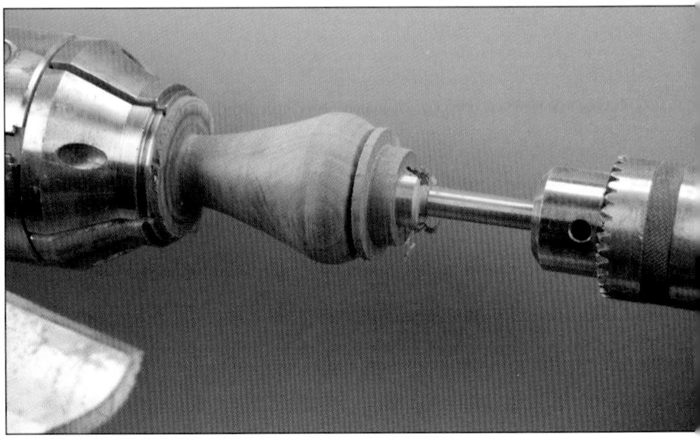

Turn a spigot on one end of the cylinder to fit the 2 inch O'Donnell jaws and mount the piece. At the tailstock end form a 1/2 inch spigot slightly proud of the blackwood opening, and form the basic shape of the finial. Drill a 3/8 inch hole, 3 inches deep on the 4 inch long stock. Drill another hole 2-1/2 inches deep by 3/4 inches in diameter, then drill a third hole 1 inch diameter by 2 inches deep. The drill holes will make it easier to hollow the finial.

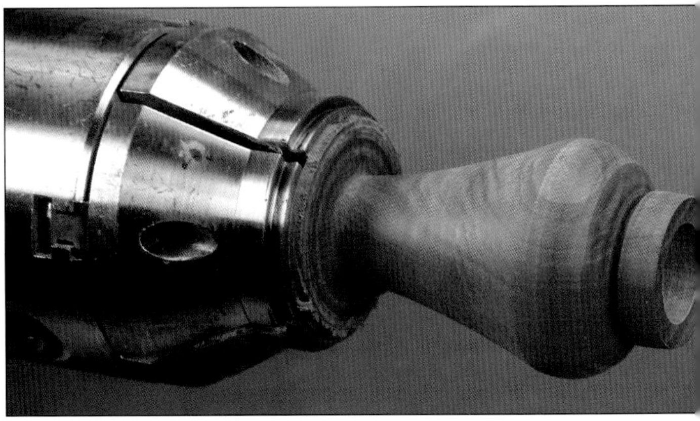

Next cut a rebate 1/16 inch wide 1/8 inch deep above the tailstock spigot, being careful not to cut through to the drilled lumen.

Finish shaping the finial's outside bottom before thread chasing the spigot to fit the blackwood sleeve.

With a slightly curved mini hollowing tool finish hollowing the finial to the desired thickness. We will have the bines more narrow at the top than bottom so the appropriate thickness must be taken into account.

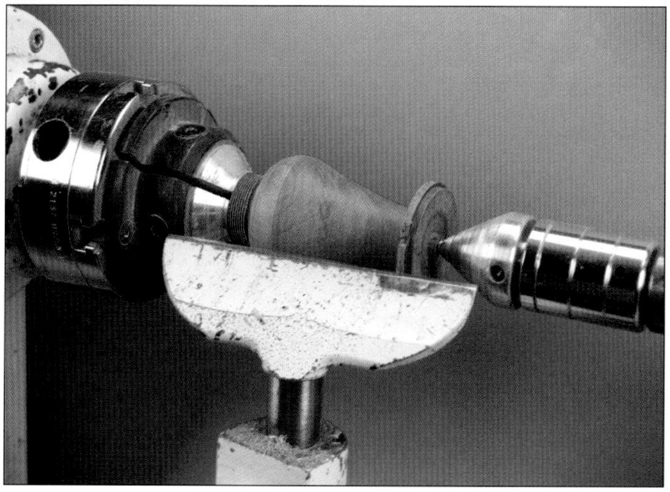

Using 1 inch collet jaws, reverse chuck the finial so that the top may be fashioned.

The next step is drawing 12 start lines using the indexer with the lathe turned off.

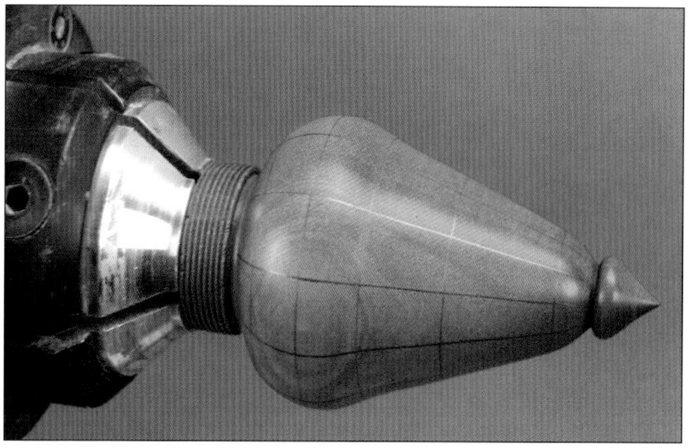

Unlike the maple burl base described above, the finial is to have colubrine bines, necessitating a steep pitch at the top spiraling to half the grade towards the bottom. This requires the pitch lines to be drawn closer together at the thicker or base portion of the pear.

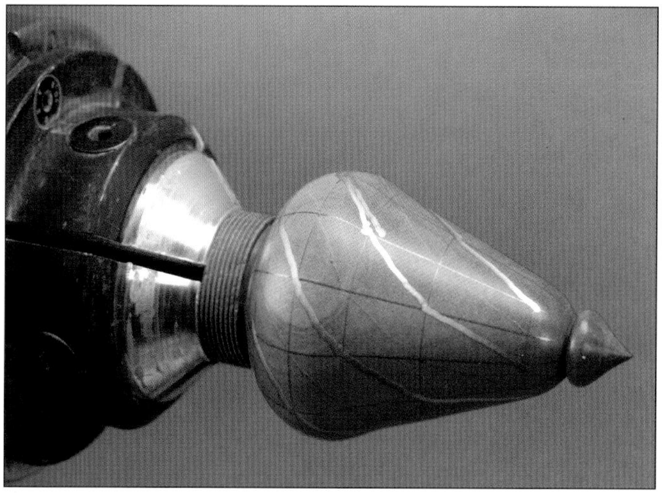

Draw in 6 bine and 6 cut lines, using an easily discernable silver Sharpie.

With the spindle locked, use both hands to cut carefully through at the bottom of the pear with the adapted grinder.

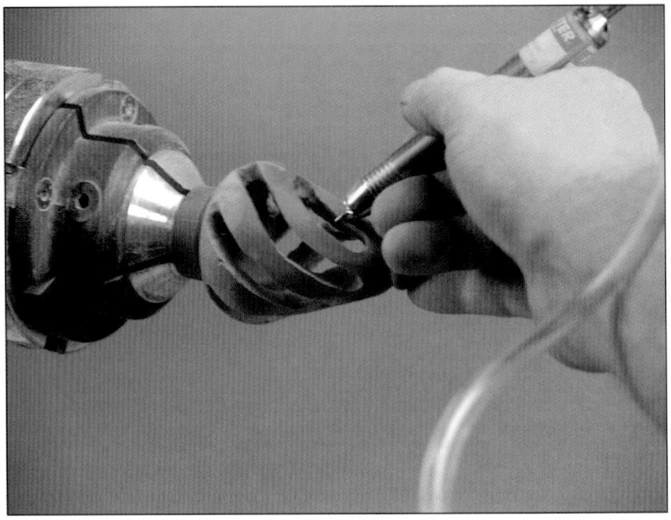

Carefully grind the undersides, controlling the bit and not allowing it to run off.

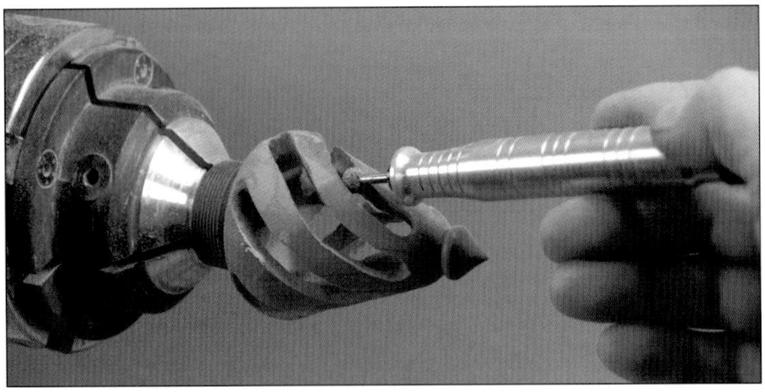

Use the tungsten pencil tipped Foredom tool to clean out the excess wood before going to the rounded tungsten tip.

Finish by using the small drum sanding tool, changing the drum frequently.

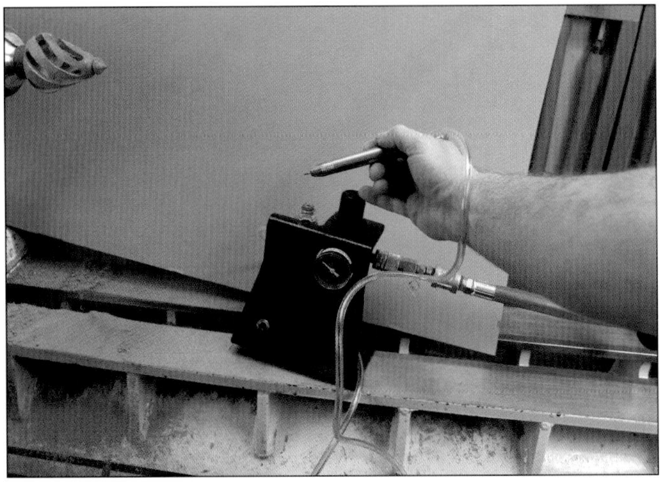

Utilizing one of the high speed (30,000-40,000 rpms) dental type air tools, finish rounding the bines, keeping the circumference of the bines greater at the base.

Hand sand with ropes of Vitex, 80 to 320 grit. Apply wipe-on polyurethane to yield a lovely product.

Two finials have been made to fit the pierced-through hollow form, the first from chapter 5.

The second is from this chapter. My preference is the former. A turned spiral of holly or blackwood could be fashioned and glued into the pink ivory finial, but I prefer it to be left open.

A quadruple open twist of kingwood with an inserted turned spiral of holly mounted on imitation ivory gives a third appearance.

CHAPTER 7

SHIBUI

The Japanese have a wonderful word with no English equivalent—Shibui—which roughly means beautiful elegance, reserved reticent tranquility, refinement, functionality and simplicity through subtle artistic but immense, non-discernable complexity in design. This chapter's gallery of finished products attempts to touch on Shibui with usable practical art and the pleasing subtle attributes of the golden ratio. It is form and function.

Nothing is more practical than a door stop for sliding glass doors. All too often a rough piece of scrap wood is thrown down making a beautiful home look second rate. The triple ribbon, right-handed twist of cherry, with a brass hinge and fastener hook, adds elegance to an otherwise common scene.

Christmas ornaments that can actually be hung on a tree are quite nice when spirals are applied. As noted in the photos this is the one instance where the plastic rule doesn't apply; use gloss polyurethane as a finish.

The hollowed banksia pod with red heart icicle, captive ring, and surface twisted sphere could adorn any tree or window.

A hollowed sphere from a recycled Christmas tree, with an extremely thin double barley twist, makes another lovely ornament.

A recycled Christmas tree provided the 7 inch long ornament of hollowed Scotch pine. An icicle of red heart with captive ring and double barley tapered twist makes an appealing presentation.

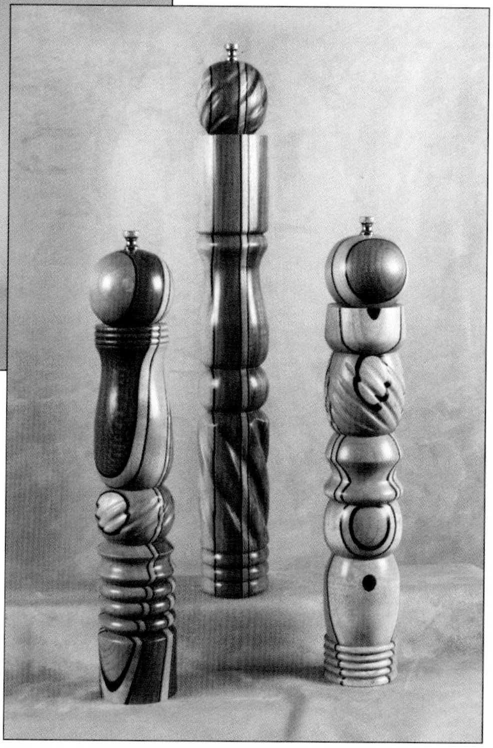

Fifteen and 19 inch pepper mills made of various thicknesses of exotic hardwood glue-ups—some straight cut and others on the bias—make excellent culinary conversation kitchen products. The diversified twists provide easy holding when hands are greasy

Right- and left-handed open double barley twisted 20 inch high candlesticks of walnut may grace any dinning area or fireplace mantel.

A close-up detail of the stem.

Decorative small compote/plant stand/pillar type candle holders may lend themselves to twists. The wood is curly maple and the stem is an inside-outside dyed veneer curly maple laminate turning with a yellow heart open variant cocobolo center right-handed twist.

Another small curly maple compote or plant stand with inside-outside turning and center post of dyed veneer curly maple laminate open variant left-handed twist of yellow heart and blackwood.

Scallop-capped reliquary of claro walnut burl, blackwood sleeve, and imitation ivory Russian onion finial.

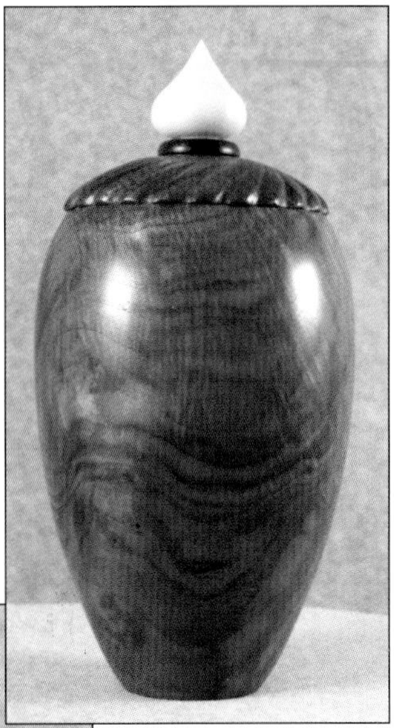

A close-up of the stem detail.

Detail of scallop-edged cap and threaded finial.

Small nested set of scallop-edged macassar ebony bowls, nested and unnested.

Scallop-edged stained cherry platter with central scalloped dipping dish—17 inches in diameter.

Threshold Series-#1, Beginning. Quilted maple, 17 inch platter with centered off-center complex inlays and concentric red heart diminishing circular inlays radiating out in a French curve spiral pattern.

Compendium of stained scallop-edged and inlaid platters.

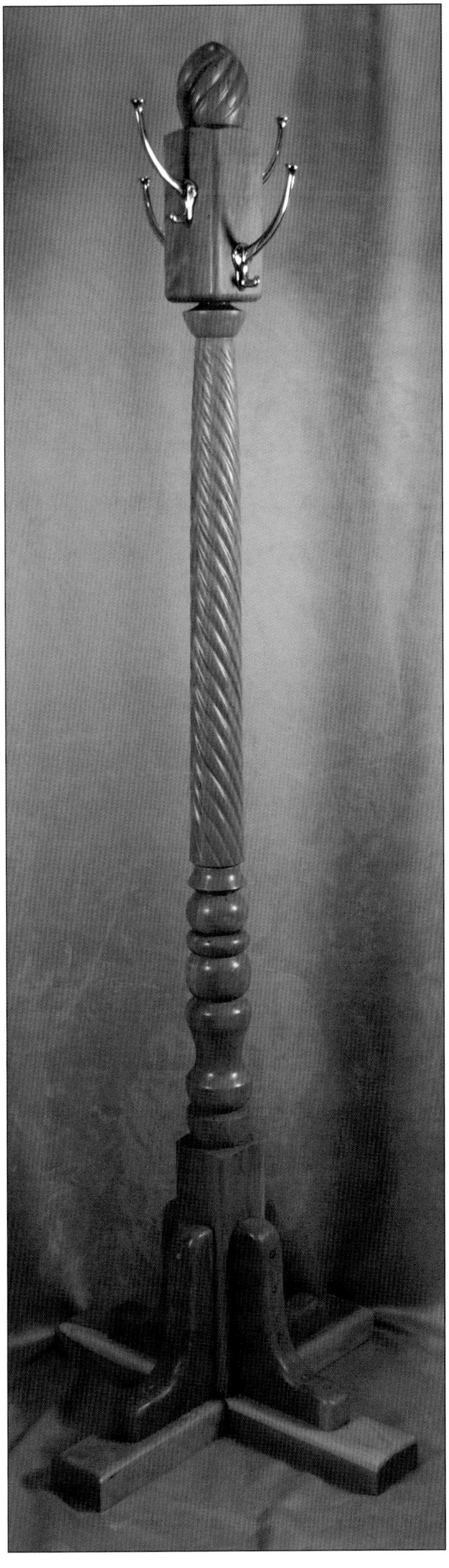

A 7 foot tall cherry coat tree with a 12 bine left-handed spiral—the base is a bit hefty as the end product was placed in a public building (church hallway) and utilized by many who weren't so gentle to the previous coat tree.

Game or kitchen table with a short twist on the legs. Notice the twists alternate right and left so that only matched twists are on the diagonal. The 4 foot diameter 1/2 inch glass top allows the beautiful cherry and short 6 bine subtle twists to be seen.

Thirty-six inch tall Christmas cactus, glass-topped plant stand of quilted/curly maple and two stained curly maple right- and left-handed twisted horizontal support posts.

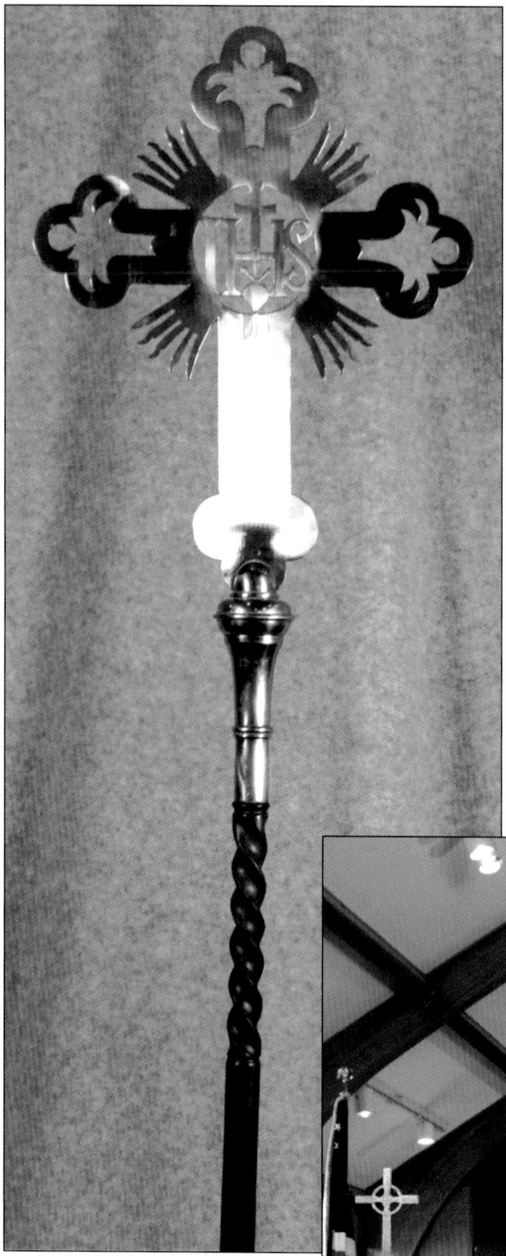

When asked, rather sternly, by my wife to replace all turned wood pieces at our church, I chose cocobolo as a rich, long lasting, low maintenance, ethereal wood. There were 2 very old crosses needing remounting, one over 150 years old. The posts were turned to one inch thicknesses with a subtle right-handed spiral for the right hand cross and a left-handed spiral for the left hand cross so that the proper cis-isomer would be on the correct side when one entered the church.

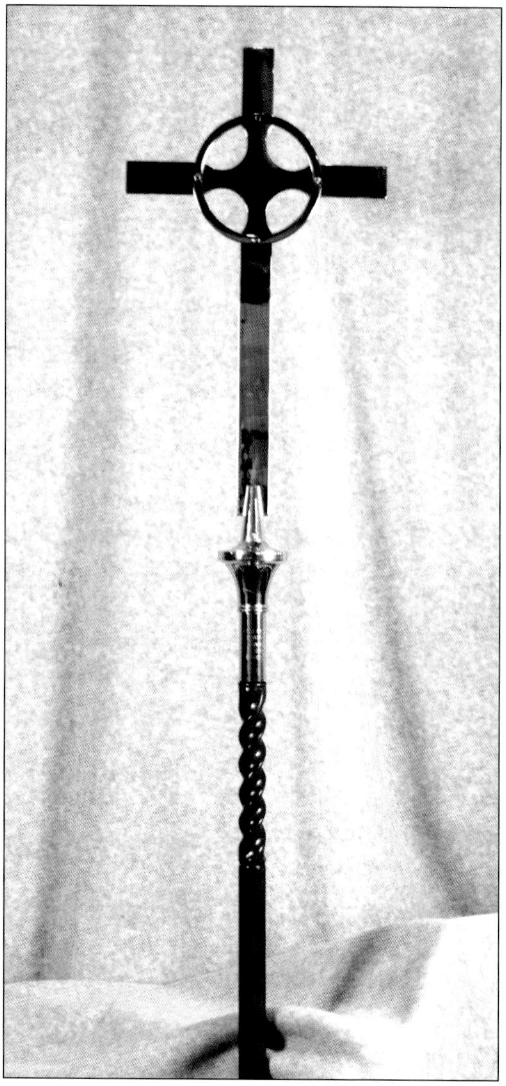

A pair of right- and left-handed, lemon wood, ebony open twist variants, with ebony dowels, blackwood disc bottoms, and blackwood Russian onion finials. The three legs, spaced on a 120 degree rotation, are of maple burl on these 24 inch high, 30 inch diameter library end tables.

Coffee table of quilted/curly maple glued together with black dyed 1/16 inch thick maple veneer inserts in the legs. The Honduran red heart twisted horizontal post is 4 foot long, bearing the mathematical relationship to the 3 foot by 5 foot elliptical glass top. The width and height of the legs match the golden mean ratio of the diameter through the 2 short axes of the ellipse's rotation. The curve on the legs is the same as that of the ellipse's long axis.

Threshold series-#2, Broken Transcription. Alaska birch burl (42 inch diameter) wall hanging/ table top with various diminishing exotic disc inlays on a spiral.

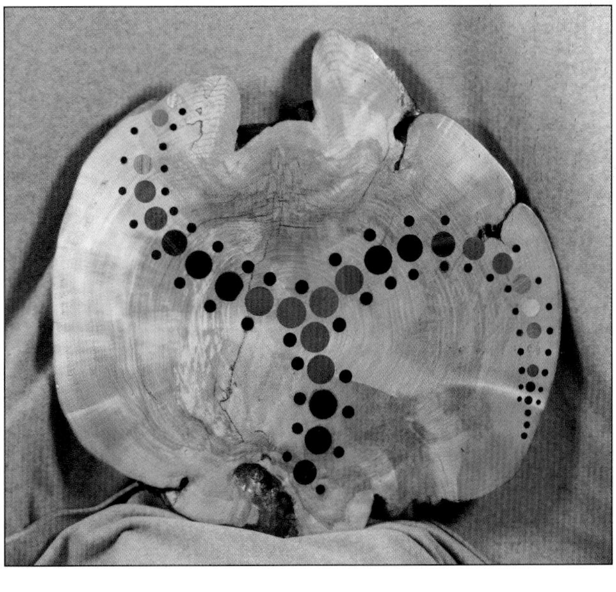

Completed 4-poster spiral cherry bed.

INDABA

It is very obvious many aspects of spiral turning have been eliminated in this book. The reason is simple. Those aspects of spiral turning the author doesn't admire or appreciate were eliminated. Many of the ornate Victorian spiraled pieces have be left out as our new age is contemporary and not Victorian. There are other old texts and explanations available elsewhere for these projects.

Techniques on how to make pineapples have also been set aside. The author has never liked pineapples on newel posts or bed posts. He recalls the wonderful story of his wife's grandmother who purchased two single cherry beds with turned pineapples on their posts. On the way home from the furniture store in anticipation of the delivery she stopped by the hardware store to purchase a crosscut saw. When the beds arrived later that day she cut off the pineapples yielding beautiful matched cherry beds to be utilized upon visits of her grandchildren. She was obviously a woman of vision and fortitude, as well as having an artistic eye.

All the pieces, save one, in this text have some useful function—the author has never been able to figure out what purpose a pierced-through, hollow form could possibly have other than a reliquary for an undesirable individual. As Frank Lloyd Wright noted long ago, great designs have excellent form as well as function. Such is the case with outstanding spiral turnings.

The most important point of this text is learning how to safely accomplish various spiral turning tasks and have great pleasure doing so. Exuberance experienced at the lathe is exceptional medicine for the soul.

ACKNOWLEDGMENTS

Without employing hokum there are many individuals I should like to thank for encouragement and stimulation in writing this book. First of all, Arnie Geiger, not only for his unselfish insistence on taking turning classes thus ending his unlimited entertainment from my turning foibles, allowing me advancement to a higher status in the woodworking world but also for his wonderful friendship. Secondly, I am indebted to the many instructors over the years who tolerated my bombastic over indulging forceful personality and sometimes sententious attitudes but who were patient enough to teach me many techniques. Thirdly, I am most appreciative of my several friends, Don Burrows for one, who read the manuscript and gave good constructive criticisms. And last but not least, my dear friend Burt Biss, whose intellectual camaraderie was invaluable as well as his expert legal advice, and Richard Acuff who occasionally pushed the shutter button.

GLOSSARY

angularly—forming an angle
assiduous—working diligently
audacious—extremely original or inventive
banjo—the adjustable base which holds the tool rest
bead—a rounded object
bines—twisting stems
bodacious—remarkable
buoyancy—relative lightness
candle cup—bowl-like structure to hold a candle
catharsis—cleansing out
centrifugal—directed outward from the center
chromaticity—quality of a color
cis-isomer—chemistry term to describe molecules that are mirror images, i.e., left and right
climes—climate
collet jaws—collar or enclosing jaws
colubrine—snake like
compulsivity—concern with order and detail
compendium—inventory
cove—a shallow concave indentation
cut lines—spiral lines defining the placement of coves
distal—away from
erudite—great knowledge acquired by scholarship
expletives—profanity
exuberance—extremely good feeling or vigor
gastroenterology—the science and study of the alimentary tract and its related disorders
golden ratio or mean—phi; 1.6180339887, a number that goes to infinity without repeating; the usual ratio used in art, architecture, or other visual presentations.
Hegemon—leader
heterogeneities—differences in kind
incunabula—the primary stages or beginning
inchoate—undeveloped
indaba—discussion or conference
insalubrious—unfavorable to health
interpolate—to insert or estimate
Jacob and Charles Holtzapffel—two authors who wrote the original techniques of mechanical turnings
Jacob's chuck—a standard drill chuck usually on a Morse taper
kerf—an incision or cut made by a saw
left-hand twist—a twist started from the left and completed to the right when facing the lathe.
limpid—clear, lucid
lumen—cavity or tubular opening of a structure
manically—pertaining to lunacy
merismatic—dividing by forming internal partitions
Morse taper—one of three sizes of tapered objects used in the headstock or tailstock of lathes, one through three
neanic—childlike
paucity—scarcity
pedantically—overly concerned with minute details
pitch—grade, incline, or slope of twists
pontification—speaking or writing in pompous or dogmatic manner
praxis—use of knowledge or skills
prodigious—arousing admiration
proem—introductory discourse
proficiency—skill
prowess—exceptional ability
proximal—close to
pseudo-aphorism—a false general truth or a false astute observation
query—question
rancorous—malicious
recherché—very rare, precious
reliquary—an urn used to house relics of a saint
rifflers—small files and rasps with curved ends used in wood carving
right-hand twist—a twist starting from the right and completed to the left when facing the lathe
start lines—horizontal lines to determine the start of twists
Steb center—a circular multi-toothed center with a spring loaded central point
topography—features and relations or configurations of structural entities
trapezoidal—having a form of a trapezoid; a four sided figure with two parallel and two non-parallel sides
true the ends—square the ends